Insiders Guide
to
Cruise Discounts

by

Capt. Bill Miller

Ticket To Adventure, Inc.
St.Petersburg, Florida

Cover Photograph - Royal Princess, Courtesy of Princess Cruises

The Insiders Guide To Cruise Discounts
Copyright -- 1990 by William D. Miller

Art by Daniel Lyons, Jr.
Edited by Mary Fallon Miller
This book was produced using Microsoft Word 5. - Rightwriter &
Aldus PageMaker Computer Software. Special Thanks to Tampa
Bay Micro, Tampa, Fl. & Professional Publishing, Clearwater, Fl.

First Printing 1990

Although the author and publisher have exhaustively researched all
sources to ensure accuracy and completeness of information in this
book, we assume no responsibility for errors, inaccuracies, omis-
sions or any inconsistency herein. Any slights of people or organizations are unintentional. **Readers should always consult with cruise
lines and travel vendors for latest prices and company policies.**

Library of Congress Cataloging in Publication Data

Miller, Bill, 1953 -
    Insiders Guide to Cruise Discounts

    Includes bibliographical references.

    1. Ocean travel.   2. Cruise ships.   I. Title.

G550.M53   1990   910.4'5   89-20357
    ISBN 0-9624019-1-9

Printed in the United States of America

ACKNOWLEDGEMENTS

I would like to thank some of the hard working woman and men who work behind the scenes to make cruising the very best value for your vacation dollar.

*Robert Mahmarian - Admiral Cruises
*Michelle Corbin & Catherine Paim - American Hawaii Cruises
*Mark Rogers & Bob Bellucci -BSL Cruises
*Bob Dickinson, Ron Horne & Jennifer Foley of Carnival Cruise Line
*Bob Wood -Chandris Fantasy Cruises
*Mike Loader & Laurdes Miro of Commodore Cruises
*Maggie Gibbs - Costa Cruises
*Patty Young & Richard Simonson,Delta Queen Steamboats
*Carolyn Speidel, Amy Dodd & Diane Orban of Diane Orban Assc.
*Ed Mass & Maxine Smith -Dolphin Cruise Line
*Bob Dolphin - Holland America Line/Westours
*Lendi Morffi & Patrice Auspitz of Norwegian Cruise Line
*Debbie Nathanso & Corrine Quick of Ocean/Pearl Cruises
*Debra DeSanti - Premier Cruises
*Andy Schramek, Julie Benson of Princess Cruises
*Dennis Smith & Karen Costa - Regency Cruises
*Russell Nansem, Rick Steck of Royal Caribbean Cruise Line
*Richard Revnes, Mimi Wiseband & John Severini
   of Royal Cruise Line
*Tony Hernandez - Royal Viking Line
*Tommy Baldwin - SeaEscape
*James Godsman & the Staff of CLIA
* Robin Cassler Smith
*Fred Mullins - Edison Executive Service   813-481-2700
*Capt. Robert Trice, Capt. Riley Bryan, Al Church, Robert Petro
*IUOE Marine Local 25
*Dr. Jeffrey Lant, Entrepreneur 617-547-6372

This book is dedicated to Charlie Miller

an inspiration to all of his friends, an American Hero
and a terrific Father.

Also to my beautiful wife Susan and daughter Amy.

TABLE OF CONTENTS

Acknowledgements

1

INSIDERS GUIDE TO CRUISE DISCOUNTS

You can save hundreds of dollars on your next cruise vacation. And you don't even need to have a relative in the business.

Has this ever happened to you?

You and your fellow passengers are having dinner on a beautiful cruise ship. Eventually the subject of how much everyone paid for their tickets comes up. There always seems to be someone at the table who got on board for a ridiculously low price. This couple says they had "inside information". Everyone else feels sick because they paid the full fare listed in the brochure.

With simple planning and a little of your own "inside information" you will never again have to pay brochure rates.

It's easy! You can save money on your next cruise by knowing about:

* The most Economical Time of Year to Sail
* Early Booking Discounts
* Making A Pier Head Jump
* Group Discounts
* Repositioning Cruises
* Saving with SeaSavers
* Sailing Single
* Standby Programs
* Cruise Magazines - Finding Discount Travel Agencies
* Buying from a Barter Travel Business

* Senior Citizen Discounts
* Cruise Line Passenger Clubs
* **How to Sail for Free**

Plus:
* 11 Reasons Why Married Men Should Take their First Cruise
* 7-Night Sample Cruise Itinerary
* Sample Menu's From The World Famous Cruise Ship SS Norway
* 5 Special Quick Reference Charts:
  - Worldwide Destination Guide
  - Cruise Guide For Children
  - Cruise Guide For Active Adults
  - Cruise Guide For Honeymooners
  - Cruise Guide for Wheelchair Travelers

In INSIDERS GUIDE TO CRUISE DISCOUNTS, each of these money saving tips is fully discussed. You'll also find **ACTION** hints. **ACTION** hints tell you how to take advantage of the money saving tips. Knowledge is useless if you do not know how to put it into action. Know How + Action = more money in your pocket.

Do you have a partner who is a little reluctant to take a cruise? Richard Revnes, President of Royal Cruises suggests 11 convincing reasons why a married man (woman) will enjoy their "First" cruise.

Cruise lines spend tons of money producing glossy, colorful cruise brochures. **INSIDERS GUIDE TO CRUISE DISCOUNTS** will show you how to read them and where to look for the small print that saves you money.

You deserve to get the best value for your hard earned money! **INSIDERS GUIDE TO CRUISE DISCOUNTS** will show you how.

Use the money saving tips to book your next cruise. The next time you and your fellow cruise passengers sit down for dinner and the subject of cruises fares comes up, Thanks to **INSIDERS GUIDE TO CRUISE DISCOUNTS,** you'll be the one with the Cheshire cat grin and the lowest priced ticket!

2

READING A CRUISE BROCHURE

Before we look at some of the juicy cruise discount programs, you need to understand how to find information in cruise brochures that will allow you to make the right decisions.

A cruise line brochure is a menu of dream vacations. As you browse through the brochure, you can almost picture yourself watching the sunsets from the decks. Or maybe you are being pampered by the handsome attentive waiters in the dining room

You will be jarred back to reality when you reach the pages that list cruise prices.

Cruise fare pages are confusing. On these pages you will discover the cost of your dreams. You need to become a detective as you sift through the information scattered about this page.

Before we try figuring out how to read the cruise fare page, let's look at how cruise lines price their cabins.

In the days before air conditioning, the premium cabins were the large outside cabins on the top decks. These cabins offered the passengers the best ventilation. The inside cabins in the center of the ship were small, hot and stuffy.

Today, all cruise ships are air conditioned. Most of the cabins on new ships are the same size. The cabins for new ships are pre-fabricated in a factory and then lowered into the cruise ship's hull at the shipyard.

Today when you book a cruise, **you are paying for the location**

of the cabin. (How convenient it is to the public rooms)

You will pay extra for a cabin with a **porthole.** Outside Cabins have a porthole, Inside Cabins do not have a porthole.

This list show how cruise lines price their cabins, with number 1 being most expensive:

1. Outside Cabins on Top Decks
2. Outside Cabins Lower Decks
3. Inside Cabins on Top decks
4. Inside Cabins on Lower decks

* One thing to keep in mind, all cabins reach the port at the same time!

HOW MUCH WILL THE CRUISE COST...

You've picked out a cruise that looks pretty good to you and now it's time to figure out how much it costs.

Open your brochure and turn to the page with the schedule of cruise fares. You'll find a confusing chart consisting of numbers, colors and dates.

No problem, this page is easy to understand once you know what your looking for. You will save money by knowing how to read this page intelligently.

THE SCHEDULE OF FARES CHART

This chart shows how much is being charged for each type of cabin on the ship.

A cruise ship is divided into cabin categories. (types of cabins) The categories are then given a number and a color code designation.

The category's color code makes it easier for you to find that particular type of cabins when you look at the ships deck plans in the brochure. The category's number will makes it easier for you to describe the type of cabin you'd like when you make your reservation.

PRICES

The prices listed in brochures are per person and are based on double occupancy. (2 people in a cabin) There are usually two different prices listed, On Season and Off Season.

ON SEASON & OFF SEASON

Here is where you will find information about the weeks of the year that the cruise line charges ON SEASON rates and OFF SEASON rates. You will find the best rates are available during OFF SEASON.

SINGLE PASSENGERS

If the ship has single passenger cabins, they will be listed in the chart. Otherwise, information about single passenger rates and cabin share programs are printed next to the chart.

PORT TAX

Always look for the PORT TAX. This fee is in addition to your cruise fare that is listed in the fares chart. Each passenger must pay the port tax. You will need to know the port tax in order to figure the total cost of your cruise.

CRUISE ONLY TRAVEL ALLOWANCE

Many cruise lines include your air transportation in the cruise price listed in the chart. If you do not need the air transportation, you can deduct the travel allowance from the fare listed in the chart.

ACTION TIP: This is the page where many cruise lines list discount programs: Senior Discounts, Early Booking Discounts, Honeymoon Specials and Roommate Share Programs etc. More about these programs later in the book.

THE FINE PRINT...
The General Information Page

The general information page is found at the back of the brochure. The general information page explains the conditions under which the cruise line is selling you the cruise ticket. The most important item in the entire brochure is on this page, the cancellation and refund policy.

Cancellation & Refund Policy

It is very important that you understand the cancellation and refund policy of the cruise line before you book your cruise. Read the cancellation terms closely. Cruise lines are very strict about their cancellation policy.

Cancellation Insurance

Most lines offer cruise cancellation insurance. You should consider buying this insurance, especially if you are planning to book your cruise several months in advance.

Other information you will find....

Travel Medical Insurance

Special Medical emergency insurance is available from independent insurance companies. Medicare and many private insurance plans do not cover any expenses you have aboard ship or outside of the US. Travel medical insurance costs $29 to $90 per person, depending on the length of the cruise.

Other information you will find...

Dining Room schedules and special diet information.

Tipping Policy, Tipping is voluntary on most lines. Most cruise lines recommend that each passenger tip their Cabin Steward $2.50 per day, Waiter $2.50 per day and Busboy $1.25 per day. This brings your tip total to $43.75 for the week and these guys earn every penny of it.

Clothing - Explains what you should pack.

Shore Excursions, Parking, Electrical appliances, Credit Cards, Cablegrams & Mail, Parking

The time you may begin boarding the ship and information about debarkation.

Vaccinations - None are required in the Caribbean.

Proof of Citizenship: If you are an American citizen you need to present a Passport or a birth certificate or a copy of your birth certificate embossed with raised seal. Some cruise lines will accept a voters ID card. Carry your proof of citizenship with you when you check in at the cruise terminal.

If you're going to the Orient or to some other exotic destination this section may have any extra requirements.

THIS IS IMPORTANT

You must be able to prove your citizenship to the satisfaction of US immigration when you return. If you canot prove yo
will not be allowed to get off the ship.

I recommend that you get a Passport. The entry and exit stamps of the different countries are fun to collect. The US passport is a powerful document to have in your pocket as you tour the world. A passport is cheap insurance against trouble at international borders.

Now let's move on to the fun business of saving money on your next cruise vacation.

3

GOOD TIMING = BIG SAVINGS!

When is the best time of year to sail on cruise ships?

You can save BIG by traveling during the OFF SEASON. Cruise lines have a hard time filling up their cabins during certain months of the year. Slow selling sailing dates often means discount rates. You can save money by planning your cruise during the OFF SEASON.

The reason for the OFF SEASON is simple. The OFF SEASON is just an inconvenient time for much of the public to travel.

Until the tourist seson begins, the cruise lines are stuck with a lot of empty cabins. That's good news for you. The savvy traveller knows that sailing OFF SEASON does not mean an inferior vacation. On the contrary, sailing during the OFF SEASON has several advantages.

THE OFF SEASON TRAVELER
Sailing during the OFF SEASON has several advantages:
* Same quality cruise for a cheaper price.
* Ships may sail with fewer passengers.
* You will be less crowded aboard the ship.
* You will receive more personal attention from the crew.
* You will have shorter lines to contend with.
* You will have a better chance at getting the best seats for shows.
* Shore excursions are less crowded.
* More deck space by the pool.
* Better chance for an upgrade on your cabin.

WHEN ARE THE OFF SEASON RATES?

* The first two weeks of January
* After Easter and all of May
* Labor Day Weekend through the first 2 weeks of December

MONEYSAVING CRUISE TIP CALENDAR

Keep this guide handy for planning your next cruise.

JANUARY: The first 3 weeks of January are a tough time for the cruise lines. People are still recovering from the holidays. Cruise lines are usually begging for passengers at this time.

* Look for NCL to offer "SeaSaver" rates. Watch for SeaSaver rates to open up in early December for January sailing dates. (SeaSaver rates open up 30 days before the sailing date.)

FEBRUARY: **ON SEASON,** February is a tough month for good deals. Check into joining a group for group rates.

* Last chance for 3 month EARLY BOOKING DISCOUNT on May transition cruises sailing from Caribbean to Alaska for summer.

MARCH: **ON SEASON,** March is a very popular cruise month. Your best chance for a cruise deal is with Early Booking Discounts. (Make your Early booking in advance, say in December.) Check into joining a group for low group rates.

* Plan for 3 month Early Booking Discounts on July cruises.

* Mediterranean - Look for OFF SEASON rates on Venice Simplon Orient Express cruises to Greece & Turkey.

APRIL: ON SEASON / OFF SEASON - April is a borderline month. Rates drop and empty cabins start showing up about 2 weeks after Easter or towards the end of April.

* Romance flourishes on Singles Cruises!

* Last chance for 3 month Early Booking Discount on popular July Caribbean cruises.

* Plan for 3 month Early Booking Discounts on August Cruises

MAY: OFF SEASON - Prior to Memorial Day Weekend; then rates usually increase. Possible SeaSavers, but these go quick. Be sure to call about SeaSaver rates exactly 30 days before sailing date.

* Bermuda - OFF SEASON

* Last chance for 3 month Early booking discounts on August cruises.

JUNE: OFF SEASON / ON SEASON - June, like April, is a borderline month. The first two weeks are usually OFF SEASON.

CAUTION: Many cruise lines reserve this time for student cruises. The ships have a high percentage of student passengers aboard. Beware of 24hr partying, noise and youthful exuberance!

* Bermuda - First two weeks are OFF SEASON

* Take advantage of Early booking savings on September Alaska transition cruises South to Caribbean. Make arrangements now and save.

The second two weeks of June become On-Season as families begin summer cruise vacations. SeaSavers are rare. Plan ahead with early booking discounts or join group departures for best rates.

JULY: ON SEASON - SeaSavers are rare. Plan ahead with early booking discounts or join group departures.

AUGUST: ON SEASON - Cabin space begins to become available during the last week of August. Try calling for SeaSavers if you can sail the last two weeks in August. Call exactly 30 days before the date you want to sail. Keep trying if you don't get aboard. Sometimes group space is returned to the cruise line unsold, and you may get a bargain.

* LAST WEEK OF AUGUST IS THE BEGINNING OF THE OFF SEASON.

SEPTEMBER: OFF SEASON - YEAH!!! Fall is the slowest selling season of the year for cruise lines. Prices sink like a leaky boat on Labor Day Weekend. The kids have to go back to school and the snowbirds have not flown south for the winter yet. Pack your bags and prepare to sail. Cruise lines will practically give away the cruise to get you on board.

* Alaska- OFF SEASON

* Bermuda - OFF SEASON all month

* Mexican Riviera - Good chance for discounts on transition cruises heading south from Alaska to Acapulco.

* Trans-Panama Canal - Alaska's cruise ship begin to make transition cruises south through the Panama Canal. Look for last minute deals on transition cruises.

* Last chance for 3 month Early Booking Discounts on December Holiday cruises.

OCTOBER: OFF SEASON all cruise lines!

Can't you just see yourself winding down the narrow rivers in the south of France, sipping champagne as you glide past the romantic castles. Or perhaps you would prefer cruiseing past fields of tulips on the historic canals that crisscross Holland.

Europe may seem like a long way off but don't worry. The money you save by sailing OFF SEASON can pay for your airfare to Europe. Steep discount promotions in the past have included 2 for the price of one fares.

The European OFF SEASON is early Spring and Fall.

* European River Cruises
Three cruise lines to check with about End of Season DEEP DIS-
COUNT rates on European River Cruises:
Exprinter Cruises 800-221-1666
Floating Through Europe 800-221-3140
Horizon Cruises 800-421-0454

* Europe, North Cape & Baltic Sea departures on Scandinavian
Seaways Line. Limited space two passengers for price of one. Save up
to $2,000 per couple. Scandinavian Seaways 800-533-3755

* Look for special Theme Cruises,
Delta Queen Steamboat Co. has Fall Foliage Cruises. Other lines with
theme cruises include: Admiral Cruises, Commodore Cruise Line,
Dolphin Cruise Line, Holland America Line & NCL.

* Bermuda - OFF SEASON.

* Plan for 3 month Early Booking Discount on February cruises.

NOVEMBER: OFF SEASON all cruise lines
* Last chance for 3 month Early Booking Discount on February
cruises.

DECEMBER: OFF SEASON/ON SEASON. First two to three
weeks in December are OFF SEASON. Christmas Week and New
Years week are very popular ON SEASON. Some cruise lines charge
extra to sail on the Holiday cruises. These cruises sell out early. Use
Early Booking Discounts - book three or six months in advance.

* Make plans for Easter/Spring Break with Early Booking Discount
*Watch newspaper for excellent deals on cruises sailing first two
weeks of January.

* Time to call NCL about SeaSavers on cruises sailing during the first
two weeks of January.

4

UNDERSTANDING "AIR-SEA" AND "CRUISE ONLY" RATES

AIR-SEA PACKAGES   Most cruise passengers must travel long distances to cruise ports. Until recently, many people never considered cruises as a practical vacation alternative.

In order to make it easier and more affordable for passengers to travel to their ships, cruise lines develop air/sea packages. An air/sea package includes airfare to the cruise port in the price of the cruise ticket.

Air Sea Packages often mean big savings on air travel. Cruise lines negotiate large blocks of seats with the major airlines. Buying in bulk allows the cruise line to get wholesale rates. They pass this savings along to their passengers. Air-Sea packages make cruise vacations an affordable travel value.

ACTION:
Air-Sea package airfares are frequently cheaper than most retail airfares. If you live a great distance from the port city, an Air Sea Package may be your best bet..
Before you decide that air-sea is your best choice, you need to understand about the alternative fare.

CRUISE ONLY RATES

Some passengers do not need air transportation to the cruise port. Cruise only might be for you if:

* You live near the cruise port
* Your driving to the cruise port
* You don't like to fly
* Your combining the cruise witha longer visit to the area near a cruise port.
* You may have found a cheaper alternative to flying

Most cruise lines will give you a travel allowance for arranging you own transportation to the cruise port. You subtract the travel allowance from the fare listed in the brochure. The balance of your ticket price is a "**CRUISE ONLY**" fare.

Each cruise line has a different travel allowance. Be sure to read the brochure carefully. The information about travel allowances is usually found on the same page as the fare schedules.

HOW TO FIGURE YOUR CRUISE ONLY FARE

Here is an example of how to figure a cruise only fares.

  $995 7-night Carnival Cruise
 -$200 Cruise Only Travel Allowance
  $795 Cruise Only Fare

Your own situation will determine if a cruise only fare is more economical than an air sea package. Below are some examples.

Comparing Air-sea with Cruise Only Rate

7-night Carnival Cruise Air-Sea

  $995.00 Fare per person
  $35.00 Port Tax
    -0- Air Travel Included
 + -0- Ground Transportation
 $1030.00 Cruise Fare Total

7-Night Carnival Cruise - Cruise Only You have arranged your own
air flight to Miami

  $795.00 Cruise Only fare
   $35.00 Port Tax
  $125.00 Super Saver air ticket
+ $25.00 Roundtrip Motorcoach to port
  $980.00 Cruise Only Total
      You saved $50.00 - skip 2
      spaces and go to duty free shop

7-Night Carnival Cruise - By Car

  $795.00 Cruise Only Fare Per Person
   $35.00 Port Tax
   $42.00 Parking/$6.00 per day
+ $25.00 Gas
  $897.00 Cruise Only Total
      You saved $133 - That's like
      getting 1 Day of your cruise
      for Free

ACTION TIP:
     In Miami, 4 people can share a cab to the port for $25 or $6 apiece.
Most of the air traffic coming into Miami on Saturdays and Sundays are
cruise passengers making connections. Don't be shy about sharing a
cab for the 15 minute ride to the Port of Miami.

ALTERNATIVES TO STRAIGHT AIR-SEA PACKAGES

PRE & POST CRUISE LAND PACKAGES
     All of the cruise lines offer packages that can extend your
vacation before and after the cruise. Special air arrangements are
included.

     If you don't want to buy the extended vacation package offered
by the cruise lines, but still want to stay a few extra days, you might have
your travel agent ask the air line participating in the air-sea program

about stopovers.

STOPOVERS

Some airlines allow stopover privileges in the state your cruise port is located. This is usually permitted on the return portion of your vacation. You should make arrangements at least 45 days in advance if possible. You are responsible for any additional charges the airlines make for stopovers.

EARLY ARRIVAL & AIR-SEA PACKAGE TRAVEL

Some airlines allow you to arrive the day before your cruise for an extra fee. Cruise line policy vary, check your brochure and have your travel agent contact the cruise lines air-sea dept.

DRIVING YOUR CAR; TO THE PORT

Parking at cruise ports averages $5-$6 a-day. Cruise port security is very tight. In Miami, the cruise port is located on Dodge Island. ($6.00 per day) You can only get to the island by crossing over a draw-bridge. Your car will be safe, there is a Sheriff's department sub-station right next to the cruise passenger parking lot. U.S. Customs maintains a 24hr watch over the entire island.

DRIVE FOR AN AUTO TRANSPORT COMPANY

"WANTED: Safe drivers to drive automobile to Florida"

Looking for a free ride. You should consider driving a car for an auto transport company.

Automobile transport companies do a huge business of driving cars to and from Florida. Thousands of people who spend their winters in Florida hate to make the long drive. They hire auto transport companies to safely drive their car and have it waiting for them in Florida.

Automobile transport companies are always looking for safe drivers. You do not need a special drivers license, your regular diver's permit is all that is necessary. Drivers are not usually paid a fee. However the auto transport company will give you a gas allowance and they will allow you a comfortable number of days to safely make the trip.

Driving for an auto transport company is a nice way to see the country, and there is no wear and tear on you own car

You can locate these companies by looking in the yellow pages under ''Automobile Transporters & Drive-Away Companies''.

5

PAST PASSENGER CLUBS

Just imagine - You've arrived at the Port of Miami. Within hours you will be sailing on your favorite cruise line.

Crowds of passengers pour into the cruise terminal. Your limousine driver skillfully dodges the traffic and delivers you to the cruise terminal's front door.

A porter takes your luggage. You nonchalantly walk past the long lines in front of the passengers check-in counter. You wait in no line. You simply present your tickets to the smiling agent at the exclusive VIP check-in desk.

The other passengers, who wait in long lines, try to figure out which celebrity you are. Have they seen you in "People Magazine?"

The cruise agent quickly hands you your documents. "Thank you Mrs. and Mr._____. It's so nice to have you sailing with us again."

But wait, that's not all!

In your cabin you find a colorfully wrapped basket of fresh fruit. A note attached reads, "Bon Voyage To Our Honored Guest!"

Inside a small white envelope on the writing desk is an engraved invitation. The Captain is hosting a special champagne cocktail party in your honor!

The ship sails and you're having a marvelous time. the second night of your cruise, you receive another invitation. "The Captain requests the pleasure of your company at his table for this evening's dinner." What will you wear? Your regular dining companions will be green with envy!

Does this sound too unbelievable to happen to you? Did the ship's staff mistakenly confuse you with the new owner?

Certainly not! The staff knows exactly who you are. And the President of the cruise line has given strict orders for you to be treated like royalty. Why the special treatment?

You are a past passenger and a member of the cruise line's Past Passengers Club. **PASSENGER CLUB MEMBERS FREQUENTLY RECEIVE EXCELLENT BENEFITS AND CRUISE DISCOUNTS!**

Past passengers often receive preferred treatment. Some of the on-board ship advantages might include: express check-in, private cocktail parties, gifts in your cabin, dining at the Captain's Table, cabin assignment upgrades and free shore excursions.

Past passenger clubs have caught the attention of many cruise line marketing departments. CARNIVAL CRUISE LINE, for example sailed with over 75,000 repeat passengers in 1988.

Jim Kissel, Senior Vice President of Sales and Marketing for ROYAL CARIBBEAN CRUISE LINE, comments that "Royal Caribbean Cruise Line does a repeat passenger business that ranges from 30% to 50%. Repeat passengers are very important to us. You better believe we will go the extra mile to treat repeat passengers special."

The purpose of passenger clubs is simple: pamper, coddle and spoil the repeat passenger. Develop passenger loyalty and cultivate a lifetime of business.

PAST PASSENGER BENEFITS

NEWSLETTERS:

Cruise Lines use newsletters & magazines to "keep in touch". Carnival Cruise Line distributes a forty-two page magazine called "Currents." Like most passenger club publications, Currents features cruise ship itinerary changes, shore excursions information. Currents also has "behind the scenes" articles about the Carnival Cruise family; its officers, crew, ships and fellow passengers.

Costa Cruise publishes a magazine called "Costa Club". You'll find delicious recipes and discount coupons.

DISCOUNT COUPONS

Most newsletters include Discount Coupons/Discount Offers. The discounts are available to club members only. These discounts are for transition cruises and slow selling cruises during the OFF SEASON.

Princess Cruises, Paquet Cruises and BSL Cruises sometimes have special reduced rate cruises for club members.

This discreet marketing of discounts to past passengers allows the company to fill empty cabins on slow selling dates, while maintaining higher brochure rates for the general public.

Just before this book was sent to the printer I received NCL's passenger club newsletter "Embark". Inside were $600 discount coupons on the Skyward and Starward. There was also an upgrade coupon for a suite on the SS Norway. If you booked a cabin in category 2, 3 or 4 they would upgrade you to a suite. The upgrade is worth a potential savings of up to $4,300 for 2 people.

ACTION TIP: GET YOUR NAME ON CRUISE LINE MAILING LISTS

* If you have sailed on any cruise line and are not receiving direct mail from that line, write to them. Ask to join their passenger club and to be put on their mailing list.

ACTION TIP: WHEN CALLING FOR INFORMATION/RESERVATIONS

* If you are a repeat passenger **always** have your travel agent tell the cruise line reservation agent that **you are a past passenger!** Even if you are just calling for information, the cruise line may offer you a preferred rate.

* When you book a cabin have your agent mention that you are a past passenger. You will want to be eligible for any possible cabin assignment upgrade. Being a repeat passenger gives you a better chance if upgrades are available.

* The cruise line needs to know about your past passenger status so that you'll receive all of the benefits available to past passengers.

CRUISE LINE BENEFITS FOR PAST PASSENGERS

ADMIRAL CRUISES: No organized club; possible upgrades or discounts. Be sure to mention that you are a past passenger when you book.

BSL CRUISES (formerly Bermuda Star Line): ''Passport Club'' Newsletter is called ''Telegraph,'' VIP check-in, special membership cruises, cocktail party, possible cabin upgrades, frequent cruiser medallions, discounts. Passport Club, 1086 Teaneck Rd., Teaneck, N.J. 07666

CARNIVAL CRUISE LINE: No organized club; ''Currents'' magazine is mailed three times a year, (Fall, Winter, Spring,) to past passengers. Subscription is free for first year after your cruise. Renewal is available for a nominal fee. Cruise Passenger Network, 2001 W. Main St., Stamford, Ct. 06902

COMMODORE CRUISE LINE: ''Club Commodore'' Membership fee of $25.00 includes: Amenities package, champagne and fruit basket in your cabin; T-shirts; sun visor; travel bag; sewing kit; luggage tags; private cocktail party; sometimes invited to dine with Captain; discounts on selected shore excursions; possible discounts on selected cruises. Club Commodore, 1007 N. America Way, Miami, Fl. 33132

CHANDRIS FANTASY CRUISES: "Captain's Club" Membership fee of $25.00 includes: Chandris Fantasy Cruise video of your choice; discounts on cruises; possible cabin assignment upgrades; private Captain's cocktail party; personalized luggage tags; Newsletter. Chandris Captain's Club, 900 Third Ave, N.Y., N.Y. 10022

COSTA CRUISES: "Club Costa" No membership fee; beautiful newsletter; discounts on selected cruises; cabin gifts; private Captain's cocktail party. Costa Club, c/o Public Relations Dept., P.O. Box 019614, Miami, Fl. 33101-9865

CUNARD : "Cunard World Club" Possible discounts on selected cruises; private Captain's cocktail party, newsletter.

CUNARD/NAC: "Fjord Club" Possible discounts on selected cruises, private Captain's cocktail party; newsletter.

DELTA QUEEN STEAMBOATS: "Mark Twain Association" Newsletter called "Calliope," features discounts on cruises; private Captains cocktail party. Mark Twain Association, #30 Robin Street Wharf, New Orleans, La. 70130

DOLPHIN CRUISE LINE: "Club Dolphin" Membership fee $19 Includes: newsletter; discounts on selected cruises; cabin gifts; private Captain's cocktail party, dining at Captains table. Club Dolphin, 1007 N. America Way, Miami, Fl. 33132

EPIROTIKI: No organized club. Direct mail; possible cabin upgrade; cabin gifts; dine at Captain's table; VIP check-in; discounts on selected cruises; discounts on shore excursions. Epirotiki, 551 Fifth Ave. Suite 605, N.Y., N.Y. 10176.

EXPRINTER CRUISES: (European River Boats) Possible discounts on selected cruises; possible cabin upgrades; cabin gifts; private Captain's cocktail party; dine at Captain's table. Exprinter Cruises, 500 Fifth Ave, N.Y., N.Y. 10110

HOLLAND AMERICA LINE: Possible cabin upgrades; private Captain's cocktail party; possible dining at Captain's table; direct mail offers discounts on selected cruises. Holland America, Attention: Alumni Discount Mailings, 300 Elliot Ave W.; Seattle, WA. 98119.

NORWEGIAN CRUISE LINE: "Embark" is a newsletter which is mailed to past NCL's past passengers. Embark features current information on ship itineraries, items of interest and special discounts on selected cruises. Embark, P.O. Box 229090, Hollywood, Fl. 33022-9090

OCEAN & PEARL CRUISES: "Ocean Club" magazine published twice a year; occasional special rates on selected sailings, special invitations to new cruise itineraries; cabin gifts; champagne; private cocktail party with Captain.

PAQUET FRENCH CRUISES: "Paquet Club" possible cabin upgrades, special private club cruises; cabin gifts; private Captain's cocktail party, dining at Captain's table. Paquet Club, 240 South County Rd., Palm Beach, Fl. 33480

PRINCESS CRUISES: "Circolo del Comandante" (Captain's Circle.) In 1989 Sitmar Cruises merged with Princess. All former Sitmar and Princess passengers are eligible for membership. Free membership includes: VIP express check-in; complimentary champagne and lead crystal champagne flutes; invitation only Circolo/Captain's parties. Princess will give you a free on-board photo. Princess newsletter "Circolo News" 3 times a year. In the newsletter, look for information on special club cruises and discount coupons. Possible discounts on shore excursions. Princess Cruises, Circolo del Comandante, 10100 Santa Monica Blvd. Suite 1800, Los Angles, Ca. 90067

ROYAL CARIBBEAN CRUISE LINE: "Viking Crown Cruise Club" Newsletter is published twice a year (Spring/Fall.) Special discounts on designated cruises; private Captain's cocktail party. Viking Crown Cruise Club, 903 S. America Way, Miami, Fl. 33132

REGENCY CRUISE LINE: Past passengers sometimes receive upgrades when they are available.

ROYAL CRUISE LINE: "Odyssey Club" Newsletter; Special discounts on designated cruises; Free shore excursions on some cruises; $50.00 shipboard credit for bars or boutiques, Free air on many sailings; possible cabin assignment upgrades based on availability; private Captain's cocktail party.

PREMIER CRUISE LINE: "Star/Ship Family" First Cruise members receive welcome letter, Star/Ship Family Passport and two Star/Ship Family Luggage stickers. Second Cruise - two Star/Ship luggage tags. Third Cruise - complimentary bottle of champagne. Fourth Cruise - Four Complimentary photos and beautiful photo album. If you sail more then four times you become a member of the "Captain's Club". You receive discounts on merchandise and upgrade to best cabin available at time of check-in. You may be asked to dine with Captain and receive a special personally inscribed plaque.

ROYAL VIKING: "Skald Club" The original "Skalds" were the Viking poets who chronicled events in elaborate verse. The "Skalds" were often treated like members of the King's own family. Royal Viking maintains this tradition by treating Skald Club members royally. Members receive a publication called "Skald". This is the only place where you will ever find a lower rate on Royal Viking Cruises. Savings certificates are offered on designated Skald Club cruises. Club cruises frequently offer complimentary shore excursions, onboard parties, commemorative gifts and special Skald hosts. Skald members are always invited to a private cocktail party with the Captain on every cruise. Royal Viking Line, 95 Merrick Way, Coral Gables, Fl. 33134

SEAESCAPE: "First Mate Club" Members receive quarterly newsletters with discounts coupons. Onboard recognition includes champagne reception party, match play casino chips, jackpot bingo cards. SeaEscape "First Mate Club" 1080 Port Blvd., Miami, Fl. 33132 or 800-432-0900

SUN LINE: "Two for One" package enables repeat passengers to buy one full fare ticket and get second ticket free on selected cruises.

6

EARLY BOOKING DISCOUNTS

You can save Big Money with Early Booking Discounts!

To receive an early booking discount you must book your cruise from 3 to 6 months prior to the cruise sailing date.

Early booking discounts are terrific. For example, you can save up to 50% off of your regular fare on selected cruises on exclusive Royal Cruise Line. Princess Cruises features "Love Boat Savers" for cruises in 1990. On some cruise lines early booking discounts are the only discounts available.

Early booking discounts are great for saving money on your holiday cruises. If you must sail during the expensive ON SEASON, early booking discounts can knock hundreds off the ticket price.

And here's some more good news
Early booking discounts frequently match discounts usually only available to the last minute passenger.

Early Bookings & Deposits Are Important To Cruise Lines.

"The sooner, the better," is the cruise line executives motto.

Cruise line executives can't rest until each sailing date is sold to maximum capacity. Early bookings give cruise executives an advance measure of how well a sailing date is selling. With information on early booking sales, cruise lines can assign advertising dollars and sales promotions to boost a slow cruise date's sales.

Early booking deposits are also sitting in the cruise lines bank account earning interest.

With Early Booking Discounts, everyone wins! Passengers are rewarded with a preferred cabins, sailing dates and the security of a confirmed booking. Plus they save money with a significant early booking discount. The cruise line is happy with advance bookings because they can more effectively plan their sales.

Note:
Discounting is used to fill empty cabins. Early booking discounts frequently eliminate the need for last minute discounts.

Examples of Early Booking Discounts
 (at time of publishing)

COSTA CRUISE LINE: Book a Caribbean or Alaska Cruise and receive $300 per cabin discount. Must book Category 4 cabin or better 90 days before sailing date. Not available Christmas or New Year.

CUNARD: SagaFjord & Vistafjord World Cruises 1990. Book 90 days in advance and receive up to 5% off.

DOLPHIN CRUISE LINE: Book 90 days in advance and receive $100 per couple discount in Category 1-4 on the Dolphin.
Save $200 on the Seabreeze 7-night cruises.

HOLLAND AMERICA LINE: Early Booking Discount program on Alaska cruises. Check brochures for details.

OCEAN CRUISE LINE: On some Caribbean cruises you can book only 30 days from the sailing date and still receive Early booking discount. Other discounts offered for booking 6 months in advance, see brochure for current details.

PEARL CRUISES: Book your cruise 6 months in advance and receive from $200 to $1,000 off your ticket price, depending on the cabin you book. Book 3 months out and receive from $150 to $600 off your ticket price, depending on cabin you book.

PREMIER CRUISE LINE: Book 6 months in advance and receive a 2 category "upgrade" on your cabin. Book 3 months in advance and receive a 1 category "upgrade". (Subject to availability). **Upgrade** means that you receive a a more luxurious cabin while paying for a lower-priced cabin.

PRINCESS CRUISES: "Love Boat Savers" for cruises in 1990. A couple can deduct from $300 to $500 off their cabin fare. Love Boat Savers is "Inventory Controlled". This means that there is no set time limit on the discount. Princess can withdraw or extend the discount program, depending on how well a cruise is selling.

REGENCY CRUISE LINE: Book 90 days in advance and save up to $500 depending on cruise and category cabin booked.

ROYAL CRUISE LINE: (one of the best programs) Save from 10% to 50% off your luxury cruise. Amount of discount and booking time required varies with cruise. Royal Cruise Line also offers "Crown Credit", which is the cruise lines own cruise purchase finance program.

ROYAL CARIBBEAN CRUISE LINE: 6 month early booking discount. Up to 20% off brochure rate, the discount varies by sailing date. Check the Royal Caribbean brochure for amount of discount on the date you wish to sail.

SEAESCAPE: "Advanced Sail" program saves passengers up to 30% on 1 day cruises booked 14 days before sailing.

7

MATURE TRAVELLER DISCOUNTS

Say YES to mature traveller discount programs.

Cruise Lines are offering senior citizen discounts in order to promote slow selling sailing dates. The best time for seniors discounts to appear is during the **OFF SEASON**.

You can find the slow sailing dates being promoted with big advertisements in the Travel section of Sunday's newspapers. These advertisements frequently offer seniors 10%-15% off the regular rate.

Anytime your travel agent calls a cruise line to check on cruise rates, be sure that they ask about any senior discounts. You never know when a cruise line will decide to offer a seniors dicount to pump up sales. So always have your agent ask and be sure they check to see if any other discounts are available. Sometimes the cruise line reservation agent forget to mention available discounts, so always ask.

NOTE: Usually only one passenger in the cabin needs to meet the senior citizen age requirement in order for both passengers to receive the discount. Every cruise line has different age requirements, be sure to read the fine print.

EXAMPLES OF SENIORS DISCOUNTS FROM BROCHURES:

CHANDRIS FANTASY CRUISES: Chandris offers a seniors discount during the OFF SEASON (April-May & Sept.- Oct.) on selected ships. If you are 65 or older and traveling as the second occupant in a cabin with a full fare passenger you receive a 50% discount on your fare. ** Offer is capacity controlled and subject to withdrawal at anytime without notice.

PREMIER CRUISE LINE: 10% Off the cruise rate year round. One person in the cabin must be 60 or older, everyone else in the cabin gets the discount. You must book your cabin in category "A" through "F". The Senior Citizen discount may be combined with Premier's Advance Purchase Plan. But not with other specials, group rates or promotions.

SEAESCAPE: Reduced rates are available to passengers 55 or older during OFF Season. Check for availability on date you want to cruise.

For the latest information on available mature traveler discounts contact: **AARP Travel Service**, P.O. Box 38997, Los Angles,Ca. or phone toll-free 800-421-2255

I reccomend travelers of all ages consider joining the following two organizations. Both offer informative newsletters with excellent information on cruises that are being discreetly discounted.

World Ocean & Cruise Passenger Society
"Ocean & Cruise News" monthly newsletter
P.O. Box 38997
Stamford, Conn. 06904
Telephone 203-329-2787

Cruise & Freighter Travel Association
"Traveltips" bimonthly newsletter
P.O. Box 188
Flushing, N.Y. 11358
Telephone 718-939-2400

8

SAVING WITH SEASAVERS

If you can travel on short notice, SeaSaver fares could be your ticket to an inexpensive cruise.

Cruise line executives prefer full ships and seek creative solutions to filling empty cabins.

Norwegian Cruise Line (NCL) has developed a special program to fill these empty cabins. NCL calls this program SeaSavers. If your a flexible traveller, SeaSavers can save you money.

As NCL approaches 30 days prior to a sailing date, an inventory of empty cabins on each ship is made. If a ship has a lot of empty cabins, NCL will offer cabins for sale at reduced SeaSaver rates.

Cabins sell like crazy at SeaSaver rates. Once the ship reaches a healthy number of bookings, SeaSaver rates are then withdrawn. The cruise line resumes selling cabins on the ship at brochure rate.

NCL rarely need to offer SeaSaver rates during the Peak Season. The OFF SEASON is your best bet for SeaSaver rates

SeaSavers can be unpredictable. They can become available anytime the cruise line finds itself with a large quantity of unsold cabins.

For example, a travel agent might reserve 100 cabins for a family reunion. But he does not sell all of the cabins and returns thirty empty cabins returned. The line is suddenly stuck with a lot of empty space. Ahoy SeaSavers!

NORWEGIAN CRUISE LINE "SeaSavers"
The NCL fleet is made up of 6 ships, Norway, Southward, Seaward, Starward, Skyward, Sunward II.

The earliest that SeaSavers rates are offered is on the Thursday four weeks prior to the sailing date.

Anytime after the thirty day point, NCL may decide to offer or withdraw SeaSavers, depending on changes in the cabin inventory.

Ask your travel agent to check the availability of empty cabins on a sailing date. They should be able to estimate if the date will open up for SeaSaver rates.

ACTION:
SeaSavers is a very popular program. If SeaSavers are to be offered on a ship, the cruise line will open them up for sale at exactly 9 am. eastern standard time, on the Thursday 4 weeks prior to the sailing date. Your travel agent must call at 9 am promptly or you might miss the boat on SeaSaver discounts.

Recently I called NCL to book SeaSaver rates for a client. The reservation agent said that they had 40 calls on hold by 9 am. The SeaSavers sold out beforre 9:30 am.

Chart of SeaSaver Rates is on the next page.

NCL SeaSaver Rates in October 1989			
	Inside Cabin	Outside Cabin	3/4th in Cabin
3-Day Cruise Only*	$279	$309	$190
4-Day Cruise Only*	$349	$379	$250
7-Day Cruise Only*	$699	$769	$345
7-Day* from San Juan, includes round trip air from Miami	$979	$1,049	$625

*Port Tax Extra

CARNIVAL CRUISE LINE:

Super "C" Savers

Carnivals Super "C" Savers are marketed only to Florida residents. The earliest that Carnival opens Super "C" Savers is the Friday, 30 days before a sailing Date.

Super "C" Savers are available only on ships sailing from Florida. 7-day Carnival ships include the Superliners Holiday, Jubilee and Celebration.

Mardi Gras & Carnivale run the 3-4 night cruises to the Bahamas. You do not have to wait until 30 days out for C-Savers on these 2 ships. **C Savers on the Carnivale and Mardi Gras can be booked several months in advance.**

The new Superliner "**Fantasy**" begins sailing on the 3-4 night itinerary in January 1990. No C-Saver details were available at time of printing.

When "Fantasy" begins sailing, the "Carnivale" will go to a shipyard for refurbishing. After reconditioning the ship will begin sailing from Port Canaveral, Florida. Port Canaveral is 45 minutes from Disney World.

The "Carnivale" will be competing directly with PREMIER CRUISE LINES which also sails from Port Canaveral. Competition may help keep prices down.

9

PIER HEAD JUMP

It was a typical busy Saturday afternoon in Miami's NCL cruise terminal. Passengers dressed in colorful sports clothes impatiently waited their turn in the slow moving check-in lines.

Outside the cruise terminal, the navy blue hull of the SS Norway stretches almost a quarter mile along t he wharf. Forklifts busily load the ship with provisions for the Norway's week long cruise to the Caribbean.

Off to the side of the NCL check-in counter stood four worried looking young women. Shifting their weight from one foot to the other and fidgeting with their hands, their eyes moved back and forth like spectators at a tennis match. The women anxiously looked from the passenger lines to the ticketing agents behind the check-in counter. The leader of the group nervously twisted her scarf into knots.

The women shared the same uncertain expression that you might see on a gambler's face at the race track. The young blonde in the group actually had her fingers crossed. The others laughed nervously as the passenger check-in lines grew shorter.

With most passengers already on board, it was almost time for the Norway to sail. Some of the ticketing agents had already closed their counters.

Over the public address system came an announcement ''Last call. Last call for all visitors to leave the ship.''

Finally, a handsome young man stepped forward. Crisply dressed in a white NCL uniform, he approached the four fidgety females. His suntanned face looked sad, and he seemed to be shaking his head ''no.'' The four women crowded closer to hear what he would say.

The women cheered as the young Norwegian officer's face broke into a grin and he said, ''Grab your bags ladies we've had a last minute cancellation!''

The woman to jump up and down hollering and laughing. It was as if they had just won the ''daily-double.''

''That's not all, Ladies,'' said the NCL officer with a smile, ''Your cabin just happens to be one of our suites!''

This is a true story of a successful ''Pier Head Jump.''

It happened the last time I sailed on the SS Norway. It shows how taking a risk with a ''Pier Head Jump'' can really pay off.

These women were very lucky. They got one of the best cabins on the ship and possibly paid the lowest fare.

How did they do it? The women took a dare. They waited and purchased their ticket at literally ''the very last minute''. They ended up with a suite and paid a rock bottom price.

Risky business? Sure it is, but if your adventurous, you might want to give it a try. You could save big bucks.

Origin of the "Pier Head Jump"

Aboard Merchant Ships, crew members often did not return from shore leave in time to board their ship before she sailed. The Captain would wait until the last minute to hire a replacement crew. The new crew members would jump from the head of the pier onto the ship as she was sailing away. Merchant seaman call boarding at the very last minute a "Pier Head Jump."

Do you feel lucky? Are you adventurous? Does your vacation schedule allow for flexibility? Are you going to be near a cruise port on your next vacation? If you answer yes to any of these questions, you might want to consider a "Pier Head Jump."

2 Ways to Sail Last Minute at Low Rates

1 - Call the cruise line the night before a sailing. Ask if there are any empty cabins. Request a discounted rate.

2 - Go to the cruise port and "standby" for an unsold or cancelled cabin. The cruise lines want the ship to sail with every cabin sold. You could get lucky and get a cabin for a rock bottom rate.

Note: OFF SEASON cruises are your best bet for a successful last minute booking or "Pier Head Jump."

ACTION: Parking and Luggage: In Miami, park in the temporary area near the passenger terminal. If you get a confirmed cabin on a ship, you can always move your car to the long term lot. Leave your luggage in the car until you have a confirmed cabin.

ACTION: Cruise Terminal Check in Counters: Visit each of the cruise line check-in desks. If they have any cancellations or empty cabins ask what the rates are. During the OFF SEASON you might have a choice of several ships. By taking a small risk, you could sail on a Luxury Cruise at a Flea Market price!

If at first you don't succeed...

The busiest day at the Miami cruise port is Saturday. If you don't get on a ship on Saturday, don't worry. Ask about empty space on

Sunday's cruise sailings.

     Cruise line agents are nice people. When you are at their counter, standing face to face, they seem to work extra hard to get you on a ship. Getting you on a ship, gets you out of their hair!

BUSY DAYS AT CRUISE PORTS AROUND THE COUNTRY

PORT   **LENGTH OF CRUISE**

Miami;:
Friday .... 2-3 & 4-night cruise departures
Saturday .... 7-night cruise departures
Sunday .... 5 & 7-night cruise departures
Monday .... 4-night cruise departures

Ft. Lauderdale:
Sunday .... 4-night cruises
Thursday .... 3-night cruise departure
Saturday .... 7-night cruise departures

Tampa:
Monday .... 5-night departures
Saturday .... 2 night departure
.... 7-night departure Oct-May

Port Canaveral:
Monday .... 4-night cruise departures
Thursday .... 3-night cruise departures

New York:
Sunday .... 6-7-night departures (seasonal)
Saturday .... 1-night cruise to nowhere (seasonal)

Los Angles:
Sunday .... 7-night departures
Monday .... 7-night departures

San Diego:
Saturday .... 7-night departures (seasonal)

San Juan:
Sunday .... 7-night departures
Monday .... 7-night departures
Saturday .... 7-night departures

Vancouver/Alaska: departures - May to September Season
Sunday .... 7-night departures
Tuesday .... 7-night departures
Thursday .... 7-night departures
Friday .... 7-night departures
Saturday .... 7-night departures
10; 11 & 12-night departures scattered throughout the season

Honolulu/Hawaii
Saturday .... 7-night departures

* Consult current cruise line brochures for the latest departure information.

10

AMERICAN HAWAII CRUISES
"A-Low-Ha" STANDBY PROGRAM

Stop Monkeying around! Trade in your coconuts for a Hawaiian cruise vacation! American Hawaii Cruises has an excellent standby program. You can save big money if you can be flexible with your vacation time.

Choose a sailing date for your cruise. (Holidays are usually sold out in advance. Have your travel agent call American Hawaii Cruises. You should check with the reservation agents on the availability of cabins for the cruise date you're interested in. The more cabins that are available on your requested date, the better your chances are of sailing.

Have your travel agent sign you up for the standby list. (Book early, get your name on the top of the standby list)

American Hawaii requires a $250 deposit within 7 days after booking. Full cruise payment is due 60 days prior to the sailing date. American Hawaii will confirm your cabin 21 days before the departure date. From that moment, you'll have a guaranteed cabin assignment and departure date just like any guest who paid the regular fare.

If American Hawaii is unable to confirm a cabin on the sailing date that you want, your money will refunded. You may choose to switch your name to a new standby sailing date.

The rates listed in the charts are available during 1989 and are subject to change. Check with American Hawaii for latest details.

The rates do not include the Port Tax of $36.00 per person.

The rates do not include air fare. American Hawaii has an air/sea program with American Airlines which gives you a substantial discounted rate

Inside Cabin Rates

American Hawaii guarantees you space in category F with the chance of being upgraded if space is available.

	Brochure Rate	Standby Rate	You Save Per Person
Cat F $1,725	$1,150	$575
Cat E $1,795	$1,150	$645
Rates are Per Person/Double Occupancy			

Outside Cabin Rates

American Hawaii guarantees you space in category C with the chance of an upgrade, if available.

	Brochure Rate	Standby Rate	You Save Per Person
Cat C $1,995	$1,395	$600
Cat B $2,095	$1,395	$700
Cat A $2,395	$1,395	$1,000
Rates are Per Person/Double Occupancy			

11

REPOSITIONING CRUISES

In late April and early May,the annual parade of ships begin to make their
seasonal repositioning cruise from the Caribbean up to Alaska.

These ships will transit the Panama Canal and sail up the West coast for Alaska's summer cruise season. In late September when the Alaska season ends, the cycle will reverse as ships return to warmer waters.

Repositioning cruises offer you an excellent opportunity to sail on luxury cruise ships for discount prices. Cruise line's have a lot of empty cabins to fill. You can help the cruise lines out and they will reward you with reduced rates.

Let's face it, the cruise marketing departments are busy. They have a big job just promoting the regular cruises in waters where the ship will spend a whole season. The repositioning cruise is a pain in the neck.

This means you will have a good chance to get superb discounts. The seasoned cruise veterans know this. The majority of passengers on repositioning cruises are repeat passengers. Cruise lines frequently give past passengers excellent discounts.

ACTION:
Take advantage of significant Early Booking Discounts that are being offered. If you are a member of the cruise line's passenger club, look for special offers in direct mail & club newsletters.

Have your travel agent call the cruise line and ask if they are extending any special discounts or upgrades to past passengers.

A repositioning cruise from the Caribbean to Vancouver can take from 17 to 21 days depending on the cruise line. If you unable to sail on the whole cruise, most lines will allow you to book just a segment of the cruise.

For example, Holland America Line, MS Westerdam sails from Ft. Lauderdale to Vancouver in 18 days. The cruise is offered in the following segments:

From Ft. Lauderdale
   to Acapulco...... 11 days
   to San Diego..... 14 days
   to San Francisco. 16 days
   to Vancouver..... 18 days

ACTION: Take advantage of significant Early Booking Discounts that cruise line's will offer on repositioning cruises. If you are a member of a past passenger club, watch your mail for club newsletters which have discount coupons. Watch for repositioning cruises which are promoted as special "passenger club cruises" . This is your signal for discount rates and cabin upgrades.

In 1989, Holland America Line, Princess Cruises, Regency Cruises and BSL Cruises (Bermuda Star) were all offering excellent discounts on repositioning cruises.

Watch for discounts on Trans-Atlantic repositioning cruises. Mid April is the time when ships will reposition for their cruising seasons in the Mediterranean and Scandinavia. Cruise lines include Cunard, Princess Cruises, Ocean Cruise Line, Sun Line, and Royal Viking Line.

In May, watch for ships to reposition to New York for the Bermuda cruise season. In October, they will reposition to the southern warm water ports. Cruise Lines include Bermuda Star Line Chandris Fantasy Cruises, Royal Caribbean Cruise Line, and Royal Viking.

The Best Time of Year for Repositioning Cruises

Spring - April & May   /   Fall - September & October

INDEX OF INSIDERS HIGHLIGHTS

7 DELICIOUS NIGHTS AT SEA - Norwegian Cruise Line's new menu for the 90's

CARNIVAL CAPERS - Sample Daily Activity Schedules from a 7-Night cruise aboard Carnival's Superliner "Jubilee"

CHILDREN'S ACTIVITY SCHEDULES - Sample activity schedule of Children's programs from Premier Cruise Line. Sample activities for two age groups: ages 2-7 and 8-12

Special CLIA Cruise Guides:

* Worldwide Cruise Destination Guide
* Cruise Guide For Active Adults
* Cruise Guide For the Wheelchair Traveler
* Cruise Guide For Honeymooners
* Cruise Guide for Children

CRUISE HIGHLIGHTS

The center of Insiders Guide to Cruise Discounts has some special items that will help you better understand the cruise vacation.

First Time Cruisers: You will find this section especially interesting as you prepare for your first cruise. The menus, daily activity schedules for adults & children, and cruise guides will help you visualize your dreams.

If you have a friend who has been reluctant about going on a cruise, this information might help convince them to give cruising a try.

Experienced Cruisers: You already know about the fabulous cruise cuisine and have enjoyed pleasure filled days at sea. The following pages have reference material you will find useful for planning your next cruise.

BON VOYAGE DINNER

...board Norwegian Cruise Line!
...reat pride in being the premier cruise line to offer a variety of
...t CARibbean and West Coast itineraries. Our chefs have
...selection of special dinners from various corners of the world ...
...nt specialties throughout your cruise. We hope this special first
...irks the beginning of a memorable vacation.

CHEF'S SUGGESTION

Russian Eggs
...ffed Egg with Vegetable Salad, topped with Caviar
Cream of Chicken
Roast Loin of Pork Scandinavian Style
Garnished with Stewed Apples and Prunes
Served with Duchesse Potato
Strawberry Shortcake

Dutch Coffee
Vandermint Liquer with Fresh Coffee
Topped with Whipped Cream

WINES

...Suggested wines for the evening to complement
your dinner selection.

...lifornia Red - Cabernet Sauvignon, Jordan
...ed - Chassagne-Montrachet, Jean Claude Boissat
...ornia White - Chardonnay, Château St. Jean
...sh White - Pouilly- Fuisse, Barton & Guestier
...nch Champagne - Mumma Cordon Rouge
...ase consult your waiter for wine and coffee prices

COLD APPETIZERS
Seafood Cocktail, Creole Remoulade Sauce
Russian Eggs
Stuffed Eggs with Vegetable Salad topped with Caviar
Chilled Florida Orange & Grapefruit Sections with Maraschino
Pineapple or Tomato Juice

HOT APPETIZER
Tortellini alla Nonna
Freshly made, stuffed green and white Pasta
topped with a light creamy-herb Sauce.

SOUPS
Cream of Chicken · Consomme with Barley Pearls
Chilled Cream of Mandarin

FRESH FROM THE GARDEN
Tossed Garden Greens with Tomato
and High Fiber Bean Sprouts
Your choice of Dressing

LEAN ENTREE
The Windsurfer
Half Pineapple filled with fresh fruits and garnished with shredded Coconuts.

HOT ENTREES
Fresh Catch of the Day
Your waiter will recite today's fresh selection
Piccata Milanaise
Tender and lean Turkey Scallops dipped in Parmesan and Egg Butter,
Served with Fresh Tomato Sauce, Buttered Spaghetti.
New England Boiled Dinner
Sliced Corned Beef on Cabbage Wedge, served with Boiled Potato,
Red Beet and Turnip
Roast Loin of Pork Scandinavian Style
Garnished with Stewed Apples and Prunes,
Served with Duchesse Potato.

VEGETABLES
Snow Peas · Steamed Cauliflower

CHEESE
Arrangement of Fine Selected International Cheeses

DESSERTS
Boston Cream Pie · Strawberry Shortcake
Frozen Souffle Nelusco, Chocolate Sauce

ICE CREAMS AND SHERBETS
Vanilla · Chocolate · Strawberry · Butter Pecan Ice Cream
Coconut · Raspberry · Lime · Orange Sherbet

FRUITS
Potpourri of Fresh Fruits in Season

BEVERAGES
Coffee · Tea · Iced Tea · Sankae · Postum
Milk · Hot Chocolate

Vegetarian, Children's Menu and Selected Kosher prepared items are available.
These distinguished selections require time for preparation.
Please consult your waiter for your advanced order.

INTERNATIONAL NIGHT

...orwegian Cruise Line it is possible to have breakfast with
...cocktails with a group of civilized Englishmen, a dip in one of
...ith a fun-loving family from France. Or share your dinner table
...mopolitan couple from California. Actually, NCL is the only
...that flies the flag of the United Nations. After all, your crew
...e more than forty different nations.
...your NCL cruise to the Caribbean becomes a trip around the
...to tantalize your taste buds this evening, our chefs have
...a exciting international menu.

CHEF'S SUGGESTION

...orwegian Fjord Shrimps, Sauce Americaine

Corn Chowder Maryland

Roast Crisp Half Long Island Duckling
Served with a special Mango Sauce
Tropical Rice

Apple-Chocolate Cake with Sauce Mousseline
...his recipe originated in the prosperous time of
Russian Empress Katherine the Great.

Irish Coffee
...est Irish Whiskey, Sugar, freshly brewed Coffee
Topped with Whipped Cream

WINES

...ggested wines for the evening to complement
your dinner selection.

...lifornia Red - Merlot, Sterling Vineyards
...Côte de Beaune · Villages, Bouchard Père & Fils
...nch White - Sancerre, J Moreau & Fils
...a White - Sauvignon Blanc, Kendall · Jackson
...nch Champagne - Veuve Clicquot, Brut
...e consult your waiter for wine and coffee prices

COLD APPETIZERS
Norwegian Fjord Shrimps, Sauce Americaine
Hearts of Palm, Tomato-Vinaigrette
Chilled Fruit Cup with Toasted Cashew Nuts
Grape or Tomato Juice

HOT APPETIZER
Quiche Lorraine
Swiss Cheese, Onion and Bacon Pie

SOUPS
Corn Chowder Maryland · Consommé Celestine
Chilled Cream of Bananas

FRESH FROM THE GARDEN
Greek Salad with Feta Cheese.

LEAN ENTRÉE
The Niçoise Platter
Tuna, Green Beans, Potatoes, Olives and Anchovies Filet
classically arranged on a bed of Lettuce Leaves.

HOT ENTRÉES
Broiled Tranche of Norwegian Salmon, Sandefjord Smøre
Served with Steamed Potato
Medallion of Pork Romana
Breaded, Lemon Sauce with diced Tomatoes
Served with Pasta
Grilled New York Sirloin Steak
Served with O'Brien Potatoes
and Sautéed Mushrooms.
Roasted Crisp Half Long Island Duckling
Served with a Special Mango Sauce and Tropical Rice.

VEGETABLES
Brussels Sprouts · Vichy Carrots

CHEESE
Arrangement of Fine Selected International Cheeses

DESSERTS
Black Forest Cake · Caramel Cream
Russian Apple-Chocolate Cake with Sauce Mousseline

ICE CREAMS AND SHERBETS
Vanilla · Chocolate · Strawberry · Butter Pecan Ice Cream
Coconut · Raspberry · Lime · Orange Sherbet

FRUITS
Potpourri of Fresh Fruits in Season

BEVERAGES
Coffee · Tea · Iced Tea · Sanka® · Postum
Milk · Hot Chocolate

Vegetarian, Children's Menu and Selected Kosher prepared items are available.
These distinguished selections require time for preparation.
Please consult your waiter for your advanced order.

COUNTRY & WESTERN NIGHT

No cruise experience in the Caribbean and West Coast is complete without a sampling of American cuisine. It is just as the many different people who today proudly call themselves Americans. And is as different as the cultures and languages that make up American society. When President Thomas Jefferson purchased the Louisiana territory from the French in 1805, the Americans inherited a rich French culinary tradition. For example, the traditional Bar-B-Q is a modern version of the French "Barbe-et-Cue" (chin and tail), the Frenchman's way of roasting wild game by inserting a spit from the mouth through the animal, to the tail. Tonight you'll taste our Country and Western cooking. Y'all enjoy!

CHEF'S SUGGESTION
Fresh California Fruit Cup
Topped with Bourbon Whiskey

Chehertma
Country style clear Chicken Broth

Roast Vermont Tom Turkey
Served with Chestnut-Apple Stuffing, Giblet Gravy
Sweet Potatoes and Cranberry Sauce.

Baked Cheese Cake
Philadelphia blended creamy Cheese in a Crisp Base
Served with Strawberry Sauce.

Western Coffee
Tequila, Kahlua, Irish Coffee
Topped with Whipped Cream

WINES

Suggested wines for the evening to complement
your dinner selection.

California Red · Cabernet Sauvignon, Clos du Val
California Red · Pinot Noir, Caymus Vineyards
California White · Chardonnay Simi
California White · Sauvignon Blanc, Sterling Vineyards
California Champagne · Domaine Chandon, Napa Valley
Please consult your waiter for wine and coffee prices

COLD APPETIZERS
Nordic Herring Tidbits in White Wine
Fresh Melon with Prosciutto
Fresh California Fruit Cup topped with Bourbon Whi
Apple or Tomato Juice

HOT APPETIZER
Calamari Tubes, Stuffed and Butter-Fried
A spicy appetizer from the Gulf of Mexico

SOUPS
Boston Clam Chowder · Clear Chicken Broth Counti
Chilled Cream of Peaches

FRESH FROM THE GARDEN
Tossed Garden Greens with Cucumbers, Radish
and Shredded Carrots
Your choice of Dressing

LEAN ENTRÉE
Kansas, Freshly made Steak Tartar
Chopped Onions, Anchovies and Dill Pickles with Fresh To

HOT ENTRÉES
Blackened Swordfish Kebab
A Special Louisiana Cajun Favorite
Served with Steamed Rice

Cordon Bleu
Filled with Ham and Cheese, Breaded and Golden Frie
Sauce Naturale, Served with Stuffed Potato.

Braised Short Ribs of Beef, Texas Style
Served with Stuffed Potato, Kernel Corn
and our Special Barbecue Sauce.

Roast Vermont Tom Turkey
Served with Apple-Chestnut Stuffing, Giblet Gravy
Sweet Potatoes and Cranberry Sauce.

VEGETABLES
Sautéed Green Beans · Kernel Corn

CHEESE
Arrangement of Fine Selected International Chei

DESSERTS
Southern Pecan Pie · Hot Gingerbread Souffle on Bra
Baked Cheese Cake with Strawberry Sauce

ICE CREAMS AND SHERBETS
Vanilla · Chocolate · Strawberry · Butter Pecan Ice
Coconut · Raspberry · Lime · Orange Sherbe

FRUITS
Potpourri of Fresh Fruits in Season

BEVERAGES
Coffee · Tea · Iced Tea · Sankae · Postum
Milk · Hot Chocolate

Vegetarian, Children's Menu and Selected Kosher prepared item
These distinguished selections require time for prepara
Please consult your waiter for your advanced orde

CARIBBEAN NIGHT

This part of the New World takes its name from a group of pre-Columbian Indians known as the Caribs. It is a collection of several hundred colorful islands famous for turquoise waters, white-powdered beaches and lush tropical vegetation. But the Caribbean is also a sensual and musical combination of Europe and Africa, of India and China, and of their people, cultures and languages. Since we are cruising the Caribbean, we wanted you to try its exotic cuisine. Our chefs have prepared a selection of dishes representing different Caribbean regions. They capture the festive spirit of its people and the richness of their culture.

CHEF'S SUGGESTION
Mixed Scallops and Crabmeat Ceviche

Havana Oxtail Soup

Marinated Glazed Jerk Pork Jamaican Style
Served with the traditional Rice and Beans

Flaming Caribbean Babalu on Parade

Caribbean Coffee
Jamaican Dark Rum and Tia Maria with Freshly Brewed Coffee
Topped with Whipped Cream

WINES

Suggested wines for the evening to complement
your dinner selection.

French Red · Chassagne-Montrachet, Jean Claude Boisset
French Red · Côte de Beaune · Villages, Bouchard Père & Fils
French White · Chablis, Barton & Guestier
French White · Macon Villages, Bouchard Père & Fils
Spanish Sparkling · Cordon Negro, Blanc de Blanc
Please consult your waiter for wine and coffee prices

COLD APPETIZERS
Mixed Scallops and Crabmeat Ceviche
Tropical Chicken Salad
Served on Pineapple Ring
West Indian Fruit Cocktail
Guanabana Nectar · Tomato Juice

HOT APPETIZERS
Escargots Guadaloupe
Snails in Hearty Herb-Garlic Butter

SOUPS
French Onion Soup · Havana Oxtail Sour
Spanish Gazpacho

FRESH FROM THE GARDEN
Tossed Garden Greens with Green Peppers, Celery
Your choice of Dressing

LEAN ENTRÉE
The Coral Island Salad
Julienne of Lettuce, Shrimp, Tunafish and Musse

HOT ENTRÉES
Broiled Filet of Bahamian Snapper
Sauce Creole, Served with Rice and Garden Green

Marinated Glaced Jerk Pork Jamaican Sty
Served with the Traditional Rice and Beans

Roast Crisp Half Chicken Virgin Island
Served with Broiled Tomato and Corn Fritter

Tournedos of Beef Diane
Two petite Tenderloins with light Creamy Sauce
flavored with Cognac-Green Peppercorns, Dijon Must
garnished with Mushrooms, served with Anna Pota

VEGETABLES
Fried Ripe Plantains · Sautéed Zucchini

CHEESE
Arrangement of Fine Selected International C

DESSERTS
Flaming Caribbean Babalu on Parade

ICE CREAMS AND SHERBETS
Vanilla · Chocolate · Strawberry · Butter Pecan
Coconut · Raspberry · Lime · Orange She

FRUITS
Potpourri of Fresh Fruits in Season

BEVERAGES
Coffee · Tea · Iced Tea · Sankae · Postu
Milk · Hot Chocolate

Vegetarian, Children's Menu and Selected Kosher prepared is
These distinguished selections require time for prep
Please consult your waiter for your advanced or

CAPTAIN'S GALA DINNER

WHY WE CALL A SHIP A "SHE"

We always call a ship a "she"
and not without reason
For she displays a well-shaped knee
regardless of the season
She scorns the man whose heart is faint
and does not give him pity,
And like a girl she needs the paint
to keep her looking pretty
For love she'll brace the ocean vast
be she a gig or cruiser
But if you fail to tie her fast
you're almost sure to lose her
Be firm with her and she'll behave
when clouds are dark above you
And let her take a water-wave
prise her and she'll love you
For such she'll take the roughest seas
and angry waves that crowd her
And in a brand new suit of sails
no dame looks any prouder
The ship is like a dame at that
she's feminine and swanky
You'll find the one that's broad and fat
is never mean and cranky
On ships and dames we pin our hopes
we fondle them and dandle them
And every man must know his ropes
or else he cannot handle them
Yes, ships are ladylike indeed
for rakes them all together
The ones that show a lot of speed
can't stand the roughest weather
And that's why we call a ship a "she"
Al

CHEF'S SUGGESTION

Smoked Trout Timbale in Aspic, Sauce Verde

Cream of Forest Mushroom Soup

Broiled Cornish Game Hen, New Orleans
with a Delicious Dressing of Spinach and Mushrooms
with a light creamy-White-Wine Sauce and garnished with
Baby Leeks and served with Noisette Potatoes

Austrian Chocolate Torte
Original recipe from the famous Hotel Sacher in Vienna

Café de Française
Marnier and Fine Cognac with Freshly Brewed Coffee
Topped with Whipped Cream

WINES

Suggested wines for the evening to complement
your dinner selection.

French Red · Château Pontet, Canet
California Red · Cabernet Sauvignon, Jordan
White · Puligny Montrachet, Bouchard Père & Fils
California White · Chardonnay, Simi
h Champagne · Moët et Chandon, Extra Dry

ease consult your waiter for wine and coffee prices

COLD APPETIZERS
Homemade Country Pate Waldorf
Served with Apple and Celery Salad, Sauce Cumberland
Smoked Trout Timbale in Aspic, Sauce Verde
Assorted Chilled Melon Balls with Grand Marnier
Papaya Nectar · Tomato Juice

HOT APPETIZER
Norwegian Fjord Mussels in a Light California Chablis Sauce

SOUPS
Cream of Forest Mushrooms · Consommé Profiteroles
Chilled Cream of Strawberries

FRESH FROM THE GARDEN
Captain's Special Salad
Norwegian Dressing

LEAN ENTRÉE
The Limbo Dancer Special
Marinated Julienne of tender Calamares with
Cucumbers, Tomatoes, Cilantro and Jalapeño Peppers

HOT ENTRÉES
Grilled Jumbo Shrimps Maison
Served with Steamed Rice garnished with Pimentos
Sautéed Filet of Grouper
Topped with a light Nolly Prat Sauce and flavored with pink Peppercorns
Garnished with Shrimps and Diced Red Beets
Served on Angelhair Pasta.
Roast Sliced Prime Sirloin of Beef Dijonnaise
Served with Noisette Potatoes, Broccoli Spears sprinkled with
Toasted Almonds, Creamed Horseradish, Natural Juice.
Broiled Cornish Game Hen, New Orleans
Filled with a Delicious Dressing of Spinach and Mushrooms
Topped with a light creamy-White-Wine Sauce and garnished with Baby Leeks
and served with Noisette Potatoes

VEGETABLES
Broccoli Spears sprinkled with Toasted Almonds
Glazed Carrots

CHEESE
Arrangement of Fine Selected International Cheeses

DESSERTS
Florida Lime Pie · Austrian Chocolate Torte, Hotel Sacher
Cherries Jubilee Flambé

ICE CREAMS AND SHERBETS
Vanilla · Chocolate · Strawberry · Butter Pecan Ice Cream
Coconut · Raspberry · Lime · Orange Sherbet

FRUITS
Potpourri of Fresh Fruits in Season

BEVERAGES
Coffee · Tea · Iced Tea · Sankee · Postum
Milk · Hot Chocolate
Vegetarian, Children's Menu and Selected Kosher prepared items are available.
These distinguished selections require time for preparation.
Please consult your waiter for your advanced order.

ITALIAN NIGHT

...le of a robust cuisine that is just as varied and exciting as
...t of its own people. The cooking of the Italian peninsula, in
...ation of the different eating habits and tastes of a multitude
...ultures that range from China to the New World. It is hard
...ve of modern Italian cooking without the tomato. Yet, no
...es on one until an Italian named Cristaforo Colombo set
...World in 1492. The Italians, incidentally, call the American
...an apple" or pomo d'oro. Tonight, our European-trained
...you to their recipes of authentic Italian dishes; and
...aste of Italy and to the richness of its cultural heritage.

CHEF'S SUGGESTION

Marinated Hearts of Artichoke, Verona

Consommé with tiny Meat Raviolis

Boneless Breast of Chicken Parmigiana
...ped with fresh Tomato Sauce and Mozzarella Cheese
Served with Linguini

Cassata alla Napolitana

Italian Coffee
Amaretto Liqueur, fresh Coffee,
Topped with Whipped Cream

WINES

...ed wines for the evening to complement
your dinner selection.

h Red · Chianti Classico, Ruffino
alian White · Soave, Ruffino
...arkling · Asti Spumante, Riccadonna
...sult your waiter for wine and coffee prices

COLD APPETIZERS
Crabmeat Cocktail, Sauce Louise
Marinated Hearts of Artichoke, Verona
Chilled Pineapple and Lychee Cocktail with Galliano
Orange or Tomato Juice

HOT APPETIZER
Rainbow Rotella, San Marco
Special Pasta topped with Meat Sauce and Chopped Tomatoes

SOUPS
Tomato Bisque · Consommé with Tiny Meat Raviolis
Chilled Cream of Mango

FRESH FROM THE GARDEN
Caesar Salad

LEAN ENTRÉE
The Riviera Platter
Selected Sliced Fruits with Cottage Cheese
on a Peach Sauce mirror

HOT ENTRÉES
Broiled Filet of Sea Bass Genoese
Lemon Butter Sauce garnished with Mushrooms, Titi Shrimps
and Capers. Served with Parsley Potato.
Boneless Breast of Chicken Parmigiana
Breaded, topped with Fresh Tomato Sauce and Mozzarella Cheese
Served with Linguini
Grilled Beef Tenderloin Café de Paris
Served with Hasselback Potato and Chef's own Secret Cafe de Paris Butter
Roast Rack of Lamb, Provencale
Served with Hasselback Potato, Natural Jus and Mint Jelly.

VEGETABLES
Ratatouille Niçoise · Buttered Leaf Spinach

CHEESE
Arrangement of Fine Selected International Cheeses

DESSERTS
Napoleon Cream Slice
Old Fashioned German Chocolate Cake · Cassata alla Napolitana

ICE CREAMS AND SHERBETS
Vanilla · Chocolate · Strawberry · Butter Pecan Ice Cream
Coconut · Raspberry · Lime · Orange Sherbet

FRUITS
Potpourri of Fresh Fruits in Season

BEVERAGES
Coffee · Tea · Iced Tea · Sankee · Postum
Milk · Hot Chocolate

Vegetarian, Children's Menu and Selected Kosher prepared items are available.
These distinguished selections require time for preparation.
Please consult your waiter for your advanced order.

CAPTAIN'S FAREWELL DINNER

We do not like to say good-bye. We prefer "farewell". It is our sincere hope that you have enjoyed your vacation, and take with you many fond memories of your cruise. Therefore, on behalf of the entire NCL staff, we bid you farewell, and look forward to seeing you again on board one of our ships.

CHEF'S SUGGESTION
White Asparagus Tips wrapped in Ham

Cream of Asparagus

Veal Marsala
Sautéed Medallions of Veal, in a delicate Marsala Wine Sauce
Served with Green Noodles.

WITH THE CHEF'S COMPLIMENTS
Baked Alaska on Parade
FROM THE CAPTAIN'S TREASURE CHEST
Petits Fours and Macaroons

Café Parisienne
Fine Cognac with Fresh Coffee
Topped with Whipped Cream

WINES
Suggested wines for the evening to complement
your dinner selection.

French Red · Nuits · Saint Georges, Reine Pedauque
French Red · Château Leoville Poyferre
French White · Puligny Montrachet, Bouchard Père & Fils
French White · Chablis Premier Cru, J. Moreau & Fils
French Champagne · Moët et Chandon, Extra Dry
Please consult your waiter for wine and coffee prices

COLD APPETIZERS
Canapés from Smoked and Marinated Salmon
Served with Mustard Sauce and Cream Cheese
White Asparagus Tips wrapped in Ham
Suprême of Fresh Fruits with Curaçao
Cranberry or Tomato Juice

HOT APPETIZER
Chinese Shrimp Roll with Mustard Soy Sauce

SOUPS
Cream of Asparagus
Consommé, Amontillado with Julienne of Spring Vegetables
Chilled Cream of Vichyssoise

FRESH FROM THE GARDEN
Captain's Special Farewell Salad
Champagne Dressing

LEAN ENTRÉE
Yam Neau
Beef marinated in Lime Juice, Soy Sauce, Fresh Coriander,
Chilies, Sugar, Spring Onions and served on Glass Noodles

HOT ENTRÉES
Lobster Imperiale
Broiled Rock Lobster stuffed with Crabmeat
Served with Golden Rice and Drawn Butter.

Baked Turbot Lukullus
Garnished with Coriander, Artichoke Bottoms and Tomatoes
Served with Golden Rice.

Veal Marsala
Sautéed Medallions of Veal, in a delicate Marsala Wine Sauce
Served with Spinach Noodles

Roast Prime Rib of Kansas Beef
Served with Creamed Horseradish, Baked Idaho Potato
and Natural Juice.

VEGETABLES
Assorted Garden Vegetables · Sautéed Yellow Squash

CHEESE
Arrangement of Fine Selected International Cheese

DESSERTS
With the Chef's Compliments:
The Baked Alaska on Parade

ICE CREAMS AND SHERBET
Vanilla · Chocolate · Strawberry · Butter Pecan Ice Cream
Coconut · Raspberry · Lime · Orange Sherbet

FRUITS
Potpourri of Fresh Fruits in Season

BEVERAGES
Coffee · Tea · Iced Tea · Sanka® · Postum
Milk · Hot Chocolate

Vegetarian, Children's Menu and Selected Kosher prepared items
These distinguished selections require time for preparation
Please consult your waiter for your advanced order.

CAPTAIN GIAMPAOLO CASULA — SUNDAY, DAY 1

Cruise Director
Bill Panoff

THE MASTER OF THE VESSEL WISHES TO EXTEND A PERSONAL WELCOME TO ALL PASSENGERS, HOPING THAT THIS CRUISE WILL BE A LONG REMEMBERED VACATION FOR ALL. ONCE AGAIN, WELCOME ABOARD!

Luggage will be delivered to your room as soon as possible. If you find any baggage in your cabin that doesn't belong to you, please notify the Purser or your Cabin Steward as soon as possible.

Time	Event	Location
12:30 - 4:00 PM	Sail & Sign Credit Desk Opens	Promenade Deck
12:30 - 4:00 PM	Dining Room Reservations Made	Terraces in the Grove
12:30 - 3:30 PM	Tour Desk opens for information & Lottery Ticket!	Main Deck
1:30 - 4:00 PM	The "Oz" Disco opens for your enjoyment!	Oz Disco
1:30 - 4:00 PM	Complimentary snacks served	Funnel Bar & Grill
2:00 - 4:00 PM	Beauty Salon opens for appointments only	Atlantic Deck Forward
2:30 - 4:00 PM	Our Calypso Band plays for your entertainment	Lido Deck Poolside
2:00 - 4:00 PM	Tour tickets on sale for Nassau only!	Main Deck
4:00 PM	ms Jubilee Sails for Nassau, Bahamas!	

IMPORTANT: Fire & Lifeboat Drill - The convenience of Safety of Life at Sea and the U.S Coast Guard makes this a command performance for all passengers. The drill will be held approximately 30 minutes after sailing. Please listen for the announcement. Thank you for your cooperation.

After our Departure and Lifeboat Drill the Full Casino will open until 3:00 AM. Featuring Dice Tables, Roulette, Blackjack, Wheel of Fortune and Slot Machines! — Sporting Club Casino

Time	Event	Location
5:30 - 6:00 PM	Enjoy Pre-Dinner Cocktail Music at the Piano Bar!	Speak Easy Lounge
6:00 PM	Main Sitting Dinner	Bordeaux & Burgundy Dining Rooms

"Please check the color of your Dining Room Seating Card:
Bordeaux Dining Room: Orange for Main Sitting
Burgundy Dining Room: Yellow for Main Sitting"

Time	Event	Location
7:00 - 8:00 PM	Shore tours on sale for Nassau only!	Main Deck Lobby Area
7:15 - 8:00 PM	Complimentary Rum Swizzle Get Together! This is the perfect time to start meeting your fellow shipmates!	At The Gazebo
7:30 - 9:00 PM	Sign-up for a relaxing massage!	Promenade Deck outside the Casino
8:00 PM	Late Sitting Dinner	Bordeaux & Burgundy Dining Rooms

"Please check the color of your Dining Room Seating Card:
Bordeaux Dining Room: Green for Late Sitting
Burgundy Dining Room: Blue for Late Sitting"

Time	Event	Location
8:00 PM - LATE	Espresso's Cafe serves specialty coffees & imported chocolates!	
8:15 - 9:00 PM	Dance to the music of the "Atlantis Orchestra"!	Atlantis Lounge
9:00 PM	JACKPOT BINGO - Join us and win some extra shopping cash! We play progressive bingo with jackpots reaching hundreds of dollars! Come early for a good seat to see the show that follows! Showball game $500.00	Atlantis Lounge
9:45 PM	"Singles' Party"! Complimentary Rum Swizzles & Dancing, Fun & Games	The Terraces in the Grove
9:30 PM - LATE	Piano Bar opens with Don Hemwall	Speak Easy Lounge
9:45 - 1:30 AM	Contemporary sounds of "Rovin Jon Trio"	Smuggler's Lounge
10:00 - 3:00 AM	"Oz" Disco opens with "Tom" the D.J.	Oz Disco
10:00 - 11:45 PM	"Music Society" plays for dancing!	Terraces in the Grove Lounge
10:30 PM	SHOWTIME IN THE ATLANTIS LOUNGE - Introduction of Cruise Staff along with fun & games.	
12:00 MIDNIGHT	SPECIAL SHOW - The Song Stylings of Dorothy Soller	The Terraces in the Grove Lounge
12:30 - 1:30 AM	Late night buffet is served	Bordeaux Dining Room
1:30 - 2:30 AM	Mini buffet is served at the Gazebo	Promenade Deck

DRESS FOR THIS EVENING: Casual (Monday evening will be our first formal night!)
Movie: "Nothing in Common": 3:00, 5:30, 8:00, 10:30 & 1:00 AM

Time	Event	Location
6:30 AM	Score for the early risers! / Main Sitting Breakfast	Bordeaux & Burgundy Dining Room
7:00 AM	ms Jubilee arrives Nassau, Bahamas! Please listen for the announcements telling you when the ship is cleared allowing you to go ashore. Please carry your boarding pass with you and return to the Jubilee no later than 12:30 PM this afternoon.	
7:00 - 10:00 AM	Breakfast served on the Deck	Funnel Bar & Grill
7:45 AM	Late Sitting Breakfast	Bordeaux & Burgundy Dining Room
7:00 - 9:00 AM	Shore Tour Office opens for Nassau tours only!	Main Deck Midship

Tour Departures:

8:00 - 9:00 AM	Nassau City Tour departs. Depart, via the gangway when the announcements are made.	No Set Meeting Place
9:00 AM	Glass Bottom Boat Tour	Atlantis Lounge
9:15 AM	Yellowbird Tour	Board the Yellowbird Party Boat.
10:00 AM	Coffee, tea & bouillon is served!	Funnel Bar & Grill
11:30 - 2:30 PM	Light Lunch is served on the Deck	Funnel Bar & Grill
12:00 PM	Main Sitting Lunch is served	Bordeaux & Burgundy Dining Room
12:30 - 1:30 PM	Farewell to Nassau Deck Party!	Lido Deck Main Pool Area
1:00 PM	ms Jubilee sails for San Juan and St. Thomas! Please be on board by 12:30 PM	
1:00 - 3:00 PM	Sail & Sign Credit Desk opens	Promenade Deck
1:00 PM	Full Casino opens!	Sporting Club Casino
2:00 - 5:00 PM	Calypso Band plays on the Deck	Lido Deck Poolside
2:00 PM	Troubleshooting for Beginners & Pros	Lido Deck Poolside
2:30 PM	Complimentary Gambling Classes	Sporting Club Casino
2:00 - 3:30 PM	Churchill's Library opens! A refundable $10 deposit on books & games! You can also sign up for Bridge games.	Churchill's Library
2:30 PM	T.V. Trivia Quiz. Television Themes from years ago	Lido Deck, Poolside
2:30 PM	"Wine and Cheese Party"! Enjoy all wines for only $2.50 / Complimentary cheeses and fruits served	Atlantis Lounge
3:30 - 5:00 PM	More island music with our Calypso Band	Lido Deck Poolside
3:30 PM	Service Club Meeting!	Churchill's Library
4:00 PM	Afternoon tea, coffee, ice cream & treats!	Funnel Bar & Grill

Captain Giampalo Casula cordially invites all passengers to his welcome aboard parties!

Time	Event	Location
5:00 PM	Formal Party for all Main Sitting Passengers!	Atlantis Lounge
6:00 PM	Main Sitting Formal Dinner	Bordeaux & Burgundy Dining Rooms
7:00 PM	Formal Party for all Late Sitting Passengers!	Atlantis Lounge
8:00 PM	Late Sitting Formal Dinner	Bordeaux & Burgundy Dining Rooms
5:30 - 6:00 PM	Cocktail Music at the Piano Bar!	Speak Easy Lounge
6:00 - 8:00 PM	Cocktail Music at the Piano Bar!	Speak Easy Lounge
8:00 PM - LATE	Espresso's open for specialty coffees and imported chocolates!	Speak Easy Lounge
7:30 PM	Movie: "Karate Kid II", 7:30, 10, 12:30, 3, 5:30, 8, 10:30 & 1:00 AM	
8:15 PM	For Main Sitting } Leonard Miller Presents George Reich's "Viola Paris" / Featuring the talented "Jubilee Dancers" / Juggling Artistry of / Jean Claude Caboocster / Vivacious Vocalist / Marcia McClain	Atlantis Lounge
10:30 PM	For Late Sitting }	Atlantis Lounge
9:30 PM	Piano Bar opens	Speak Easy Lounge
9:45 PM	"Adult Disco" opens with the "Robin Jon Trio"	Smuggler's Lounge
10:00 PM	Disco opens	Oz Disco
10:00 PM	"Music Society" plays for dancing!	Terrace in the Grove Lounge
10:00 PM	The "Atlantis Orchestra" plays!	Atlantis Lounge
12:00 MIDNIGHT	SPECIAL SHOW - Swinging Sounds of Jim Coston	Terraces in the Grove Lounge
12:30 - 1:30 AM	Late night buffet served	Bordeaux Dining Room
1:00 AM	Mini buffet served at the Bus Stop!	Promenade Deck Midship

DRESS FOR THE EVENING: Formal (The next formal evening will be Friday)
PLEASE NOTE: The Port Side of the Atlantis and Terraces on the Grove Lounges are reserved for non-smoking passengers. Thank you for your co-operation in this special request.

TUESDAY, DAY 3

Time	Event	Location
6:30 AM	Coffee for all the early risers!	Funnel Bar & Grill
7:45 AM	Main Sitting Breakfast	Bordeaux & Burgundy Dining Rooms
8:00 - 10:00 AM	Breakfast served on Deck	Funnel Bar & Grill
9:00 AM - LATE	Gazebo Bar Opens	Promenade Deck
9:00 - 11:00 AM	Churchill's Library opens! A refundable $10.00 deposit on books and games!	Churchill's Library
9:00 AM	Late Sitting Breakfast	Bordeaux & Burgundy Dining Rooms
10:00 AM	Exercises for the Physically Shot! Morning Stretch!	Lido Deck
9:45 AM	MEN'S KNOBBY KNEES CONTEST. Ladies, can help us judge	Atlantis Lounge
11:00 AM	TRAPSHOOTING	Promenade Deck
10:00 - 11:00 AM	Coffee, tea & bouillon served	Funnel Bar & Grill
Tours of the Bridge	Tickets for the Bridge Tour will be given out in the Atlantis Lounge at 4:15 PM. Please be early, the tour is limited due to space.	
11:16 AM	TRAVEL TALK! An important talk about U.S. Custom rules and regulations, the next two port of calls, the Shore Excursion program and general ship information	Atlantis Lounge
11:30 - 2:30 PM	TOUR OFFICE: Visa, Mastercard, American Express, Cash and Traveller's checks accepted. The tours are limited, so please book early!	Terraces in the Grove Lounge
11:50 AM	Sun Lovers Lunch is served on Deck	Funnel Bar & Grill
12:00 NOON	Captain's Bulletin announced from the Bridge! Main Sitting Lunch	Bordeaux & Burgundy Dining Rooms
1:00 - 3:00 PM	Library opens! (Looking for a Bridge or Card partner? Sign up!)	Atlantic Deck
1:00 PM - 3:00 AM	Full Casino opens!	Sporting Club Casino
1:30 PM	Late Sitting Lunch	Bordeaux & Burgundy Dining Rooms
2:30 PM	TRAPSHOOTING	Promenade Deck Aft.
2:30 - 5:30 PM	Calypso Music for your listening and dancing pleasure!	Lido Deck
2:30 PM	GRANDMOTHER'S & HONEYMOONER'S PARTY (Complimentary Champagne)!	Atlantis Lounge
2:45 PM	Afternoon Workout for the more advanced! Please bring a towel.	Oz Disco
3:15 PM	Double Your Cash BINGO - Bring all camera tickets. If you are in the "Atlantis Lounge" at the beginning of our bingo session, you can play all afternoon for only $10.00! This does not included the cover-all. SNOWBALL will pay $1,000.00	
2:30 PM	BEER DRINKING CONTEST	Lido Deck, Poolside
4:00 - 5:00 PM	Coffee, tea, ice cream and other treats!	Funnel Bar & Grill
4:15 PM	Bridge Tour passes will be given out in the lounge...	Atlantis Lounge
4:30 PM	Visit to the Bridge (Wheelhouse)	
4:30 PM	"Galley Tour"	Entrance of the Burgundy Dining Room!
5:30 & 7:30 PM	Cocktail Music at the Piano Bar!	Speak Easy Lounge
5:15 & 7:15 PM	Happy Hour with Guacamole Special!	Gazebo
6:00 PM	Main Sitting Dinner	Bordeaux & Burgundy Dining Rooms
7:00 - 7:45 PM	Dance to the music of the "Atlantis Orchestra"	Atlantis Lounge
8:00 - 1:00 AM	Espresso's opens for specialty coffees & chocolates!	Promenade Deck
8:00 PM	Late Sitting Dinner	Bordeaux & Burgundy Dining Rooms
7:45 PM	SHOWTIME! (Main Sitting) & 10:30 PM (Late Sitting) The Insane Comedy of Bill Panoff The Multi-talented Wes Epae - Ventriloquist Bill Boley	Atlantis Lounge
9:00 PM	SNOWBALL JACKPOT BINGO - Great Prizes	Atlantis Lounge
9:30 PM	Sing along at the Piano Bar with Jack!	Speak Easy Lounge
9:45 PM	"Masquerade" featuring "Lauren" in the "Adult Disco"!	Smuggler's Lounge
10:00 PM	"Music Society" plays for dancing!	Terraces in the Grove Lounge
10:00 PM	Oz Disco opens with "Bob"	Oz Disco
12:00 MIDNIGHT	SPECIAL SHOW Vivacious Vocalist Marcia McClain	Terraces in the Grove Lounge
12:30 AM	Late Night Buffet	Burgundy Dining Room

WEDNESDAY, DAY 4 — WELCOME TO SAN JUAN

Time	Event	Location
6:30 AM	Coffee for all the early risers!	Funnel Bar & Grill
7:45 AM	Main Sitting Breakfast	Bordeaux & Burgundy Dining Rooms
8:00 - 10:00 AM	Breakfast on the Lido Deck	Funnel Bar & Grill
8:00 AM	Slot Machines open	Sporting Club Casino
9:00 - LATE	Gazebo Bar opens	Promenade Deck
9:00 - 10:30 AM	Library opens! A refundable $10 deposit on all books and games	"A" Deck Forward
9:00 AM	Late Sitting Breakfast	Bordeaux & Burgundy Dining Rooms
9:45 AM	GOLF DRIVING	Promenade Deck Aft.
9:45 AM	NEWLYWED & NOT SO NEWLYWED GAME	Atlantis Lounge
10:00 - 11:00 AM	Coffee, tea & bouillon served	Funnel Bar & Grill
10:00 AM	Exercises for beginners & intermediates	Main Poolside Area
10:30 AM	SHOPPING TALK - Learn where all the best buys are in San Juan and St. Thomas and who offers specials for Jubilee passengers!	Atlantis Lounge
11:30 - 2:30 PM	Sun Lovers Lunch served	Funnel Bar & Grill
11:00 - 1:00 PM	Tour Office opens	Main Lobby
11:30 - 1:30 PM	Open Sitting Lunch	Bordeaux & Burgundy Dining Rooms
2:00 PM	The ms Jubilee arrives in San Juan, Puerto Rico! Upon arrival... Please note: All Non-U.S. citizens, alien residents, "Canadians must check with U.S. Immigration in the Terraces in the Grove Lounge on Promenade Deck Aft. Please listen for announcements! Thanks! All tour departures. Listen for announcements!	
4:00 PM	Tea, coffee & goodies are served!	Funnel Bar & Grill
5:00 PM	Main Sitting Dinner	Both Dining Rooms
7:00 PM	Late Sitting Dinner	Both Dining Rooms
PLEASE NOTE:	The Purser's Office is selling night club tours at the window on Main Deck from 2 PM until 8 PM	
8:00 - 8:45 PM	Nightclub Tours depart! Please listen for announcements! Gentlemen must wear jackets in Casinos in Port. Ladies may wear dresses or pants outfits	Promenade Deck
10:00 PM	The "Oz" Disco opens!	Promenade Deck
12:00 MIDNIGHT	DECK PARTY - Our late night buffet is served under the stars on Lido Deck by the Main Pool All passengers are cordially invited. Limbo Contest!	Lido Deck Main Pool Area
1:30 AM	The ms Jubilee Sails for St. Thomas! All passengers are requested to be onboard no later than 1:30 AM! Please carry your boarding pass with you when going ashore. Thank You!	

IN CASE OF EXTREME EMERGENCY ONLY WHILE IN SAN JUAN, PLEASE CONTACT:
Continental Shipping, Inc.
400 Commercio
San Juan, Puerto Rico Telephone: 809-725-2530

Movie: "Wise Guys" 7:30, 10, 12:30, 3, 5:30, 8, 10:30 @ 1 AM.

St. Thomas

Time	Activity	Location
8:30 AM	St. John's Island & Corfu World Tour	Departs from Deck 3 Gangway
8:30 AM	Morning Snorkel & Scuba Tours	Meet in the Disco
8:30 AM	St. John Island Tour	Meet on "A" Deck of Atlantis Lounge
12:30 PM	Afternoon Snorkel & Scuba Tours	Meet in the Disco

(NOTE: Passengers on the Kon Tiki may pick up this tour in town by boarding the Kon Tiki Raft on the waterfront side of A.H. Rise Liquor Store at 1:45 PM.)

Time	Activity	Location
6:30 AM	Coffee for early risers	Funnel Bar & Grill
7:00 AM	Main Sitting Breakfast	Bordeaux & Burgundy Dining Rooms
8:00 AM	ms Jubilee arrives in St. Thomas, U.S.V.I.! Please carry your boarding pass with you when you go ashore and be back to the ship no later than 5:00PM	
8:15 AM	Late Sitting Breakfast	Bordeaux & Burgundy Dining Rooms
7:45 - 9:00 AM	Shore Tour Office opens	Main Deck Midship
8:00 - 10:00 AM	Breakfast is served on Deck	Funnel Bar & Grill
10:15 - 11:00 AM	Coffee, tea & bouillon is served	Funnel Bar & Grill

PLEASE NOTE: All passengers on tours should meet at the designated areas listed at least 10 minutes early!

Time	Activity	Location
11:30 - 2:30 PM	Sun Lovers Light Lunch is served	Funnel Bar & Grill
11:30 - 5:00 PM	Late Sitting Buffet Lunch is served	Bordeaux Dining Room
3:30 - 5:30 PM	Enjoy Calypso music on the Lido Deck	Poolside
4:00 - 5:00 PM	Coffee, tea & Ice cream	Funnel Bar & Grill
5:00 PM	PASSENGER TALENT SHOW REHEARSAL & AUDITION! If you are going to be in the Talent Show this evening, you must attend this rehearsal. Please be on time! The Talent Show will be limited to 12 acts!	Atlantis Lounge
5:00 - 6:00 PM	Farewell to St. Thomas Deck Party! Enjoy the sights of beautiful Charlotte Amalie as we sail from our final great port of call!	Lido Deck Poolside
5:30 PM	The Jubilee sails for Miami, Florida! All passengers must be on board no later than 5:00 PM as we sail at 5:30 PM!	
7:00 PM	The Duty Free Shop opens	Atlantic Deck Forward
6:00 - LATE!	The Casino opens!	Sporting Club Casino
6:00 PM	Main Sitting Dinner	Bordeaux & Burgundy Dining Rooms
5:30 & 7:30 PM	Pre-Dinner Cocktail music in the Gazebo & the Speak Easy Lounge	
8:00PM	Late Sitting Dinner	
8:00 - 1:00 AM	Espresso's opens for specialty coffees & imported chocolates!!	
8:15 - 9:00 PM	Dance to the big band sounds of the Atlantis Orchestra!	Atlantis Lounge
9:00 PM	PRO/GOLD BINGO - Chance at $1300.00!! Tonight we will be giving away 14 karat gold with the cash prizes! Bring your draw tickets from the St. Thomas stores!!	Atlantis Lounge
9:30 PM	Jack opens the Piano Bar	Speak Easy Lounge
9:45 PM	Enjoy sounds of "Robin Jon Trio"	Smuggler's Lounge
10:00 PM	The Disco opens with D.J. Bob Dawson	Oz Disco
10:45 PM	PASSENGER TALENT SHOW	Atlantis Lounge
12:00 MIDNIGHT	SPECIAL SHOW - Adult Rated! The Comedy Ventriloquism of Bill Boley No Children, Please!	Terraces in the Grove Lounge
12:30 - 1:30 AM	Late Night Buffet,	Burgundy Dining Room
1:30 - 2:30 AM	Mini Buffet, served at the Gazebo!	Promenade Deck

DRESS FOR THE EVENING: Casual
Movie: "Back to School" 7:30, 10:00, 12:30, 3:00, 5:30, 8:00, 10:30 & 1:00 AM
IN CASE OF EXTREME EMERGENCY ONLY CONTACT:
The West Indiana Company
West Indiana Pier
St. Thomas, U.S.V.I.
Tel: (809) 774-1780

Time	Activity	Location
7:45 AM	Coffee for the early risers / Main Sitting Breakfast	Funnel Bar & Grill / Bordeaux & Burgundy Dining Rooms
8:00 - 10:00 AM	Breakfast served on deck	Funnel Bar & Grill
8:00 AM	Slot Machines open until late	Sporting Club Casino
9:00 AM	Late Sitting Breakfast	Bordeaux & Burgundy Dining Rooms
9:00 - 11:00 AM	Churchill's Library opens!	Atlantic Deck Forward
9:00 AM	Coffee, tea & bouillon served	Promenade Deck
10:00 AM	Exercise to keep fit!	Funnel Bar & Grill
10:00 AM	TRAPSHOOTING	Lido Deck Main Pool Area
9:45 - 11:00 AM	TRAPSHOOTING	Promenade Deck Aft
11:00 AM	Pillow fighting Contest. Try your luck on the slippery pole!	Lido Deck, Poolside
11:30 AM	Shuffleboard Tournament.	Verandah Deck, Midship
11:30 - 2:30 PM	Light Lunch served on Deck	Funnel Bar & Grill
11:50 AM	Captain's Bulletin is announced from the Bridge!	
12:00 NOON	Main Sitting Lunch	Bordeaux & Burgundy Dining Rooms
1:00 - 3:00 PM	Full Casino opens!	Sporting Club Casino
1:00 - 3:00 PM	Churchill's Library opens	Atlantic Deck
1:30 PM	Late Sitting Lunch	Bordeaux & Burgundy Dining Rooms
2:00 PM	TRAPSHOOTING	Promenade Deck Aft
2:00 - 3:50 PM	The Calypso Band plays	Lido Deck Midship
2:30	JACKPOT BINGO. (No Bingo tonight) Bring raffle tickets from the San Juan stores to Bingo today!	Atlantis Lounge
3:00 PM	Afternoon Workout from the more advanced! Please bring a towel	Oz Disco
Followed by the...	Hilarious Joke Telling Contest. Each passenger should prepare one joke to tell on stage. No racial or dirty jokes will be accepted	Atlantis Lounge
4:00 - 5:00 PM	Coffee, tea, Ice cream and other treats!	Funnel Bar & Grill
4:30 PM	Visit to the Bridge	Meet in the Atlantis Lounge
4:45 - 6:00 PM / 7:00 - 8:00 PM	Farewell Appreciation Get-Together	Atlantis Lounge
5:45 PM	(Masquerade Parade Tomorrow Night.) Main Sitting Dinner	Bordeaux & Burgundy Dining Rooms
8:00 PM	Late Sitting Dinner	Bordeaux & Burgundy Dining Rooms
8:00 - 1:00 AM	Espresso's serves specialty coffees & chocolates!	Promenade Deck
8:15 PM	SHOWTIME for Main Sitting 10:30 PM SHOWTIME for Late Sitting Leonard Miller Presents George Reich's "DAZZLE DAZZLE" Featuring the talented "Jubilee Dancers" with Marcia McClain! The Swinging Sounds of Jim Coston Comedian Tommy Van	Atlantis Lounge
9:30 PM	Sing along with "Jack" at the Piano Bar!	Speak Easy Lounge
9:45 PM	Contemporary sounds with "Robin Jon Trio"	Smuggler's Lounge
10:00 PM	"Music Society" plays for dancing	Terraces in the Grove Lounge
10:00 PM	Disco opens with "Bob" the DJ.	Oz Disco
11:30 - 12:15 AM	The Bordeaux Dining Room opens for picture taking only of the outstanding displays of the Grand Gala Buffet!	Bordeaux Dining Room
12:00 MIDNIGHT	SPECIAL SHOWTIME - "Hawaiian Cowboy" WES EPAE Singer/Impressionist.	The Terraces in the Grove Lounge
12:30 - 1:30 AM	The Bordeaux Dining Room opens to partake of the sumptuous Gala Buffet!	Bordeaux Dining Room
1:30 - 2:30 AM	Mini Buffet is served at the Gazebo!	Promenade Deck

Movie: "Down & Out in Beverly Hills" 7:30, 10, 12:30, 3, 5:30, 8, 10:30 & 1 AM
IMPORTANT!!!! MOVE YOUR CLOCKS & WATCHES BACK ONE HOUR BEFORE RETIRING TONIGHT!!!!

Time	Event	Location
6:30 AM	Coffee for all the early risers!	Funnel Bar & Grill
7:45 AM	Main Sitting Breakfast	Bordeaux & Burgundy Dining Rooms
8:00 AM - LATE	Slot Machines open	Sporting Club Casino
8:00 - 10:00 AM	Breakfast served on Deck	Funnel Bar & Grill
9:00 AM	Late Sitting Breakfast	Bordeaux & Burgundy Dining Rooms
9:00 AM	Gazebo Bar opens!	Promenade Deck
9:00 - 11:00 AM	Churchill's Library opens!	Atlantic Deck Forward
10:00 AM	Coffee, tea & bouillon served	Funnel Bar & Grill
10:00 AM	Morning Stretch Exercises: Please bring a towel.	Atlantis Lounge
10:00 AM	Ping Pong Tournament for the Adults!	Promenade Deck Aft
9:45 AM	Name that Tune	Atlantis Lounge
9:45 AM	HORSERACING	Atlantis Lounge
10:30 AM	Debarkation Talk. It is very important that you attend this informative talk this morning, covering baggage handling, how to fill out custom forms, tips and gratuities, transportation, etc. This will make it much easier to disembark tomorrow in Miami.	Atlantis Lounge
11:00 AM	WHITE ELEPHANT AUCTION	Atlantis Lounge
1:30 - 2:00 PM	Merchandise Adjustments! (For guaranteed stores)	Tour Desk - Main Deck
11:30 - 2:30 PM	Light Deck Luncheon served	Funnel Bar & Grill
11:50 AM	Captain's Bulletin from the Bridge!	
12:00 NOON	Main Sitting Lunch	Bordeaux & Burgundy Dining Rooms
1:00 PM	ICE CARVING DEMONSTRATION! Bring your camera.	Lido Deck Poolside
1:00 PM - 3:00 AM	Full Casino Opens!	Sporting Club Casino
1:00 - 3:00 PM	Churchill's Library opens for the return of all books and games! Don't forget to pick up your deposits.	Atlantic Deck Forward
1:00 - 2:00 PM	Masquerade supplies available! You can be creative and get involved in the parade tonight. The supplies are free.	Atlantis Lounge Starboard Side
1:30 PM	Late Sitting Lunch	Bordeaux & Burgundy Dining Rooms
2:00 PM	TRAPSHOOTING TOURNAMENT	Promenade Deck Aft
3:00 - 5:00 PM	Calypso Music Poolside	Lido Deck
3:00 PM	JACKPOT BINGO - SNOWBALL $1500.00 This afternoon we will be collecting all the raffle tickets from T-Shirt Factory Outlet. All passengers must be present to win....	Atlantis Lounge
4:00 - 5:00 PM	Coffee, tea, ice cream & other treats!	Funnel Bar & Grill
4:15 PM	All Male Nightgown Contestants must register in the Oz Disco! Please be in your outfit! Pick up your entry form at the Shore Tours Desk counter on Main Deck Midship and have it filled out.	
Followed by:	The MALE NIGHTGOWN CONTEST	Atlantis Lounge
5:00 & 7:00 PM	"Funship" Highlight Parties! Everyone is invited to enjoy some complimentary hors d'oeuvres, bar specials, live music and dancing.	Terraces in the Grove Lounge
7:15 - 8:00 PM	Dixieland Band	Gazebo on P-Deck
5:30 & 7:30 PM	Cocktail Piano music at the Piano Bar!	Speak Easy Lounge
6:00 PM	Main Sitting Dinner	Bordeaux & Burgundy Dining Rooms
8:00 PM	Late Sitting Dinner	Bordeaux & Burgundy Dining Rooms
8:15 - 9:00 PM	Nostalgia Time - Big Band Dance Music!	Atlantis Lounge
9:00 PM	SNOWBALL BINGO - Guaranteed payout of $1500.00 with a chance to win $2000.00 Jackpot!	Atlantis Lounge
9:30 PM	"Jack" at the Piano Bar!	Speak Easy Lounge
9:45 PM	Dance the night away with "Masquerade!"	Smuggler's Lounge
10:00 PM	Oz Disco opens! The last night to visit the "Wizard!"	Oz Disco
10:30 PM	Registration for all masquerade contestants! Please be in your costume. Complimentary Champagne	Speak Easy Lounge
10:45 PM	MASQUERADE PARADE	Atlantis Lounge
12:00 MIDNIGHT	SPECIAL SHOW	Terrace in the Grove Lounge
	"Adult Show" - Comedian Tommy Van	
12:30 - 1:30 AM	Late Night Buffet Served!	Burgundy Dining Room
1:30 - 2:30 AM	Mini Buffet served at the Gazebo!	Promenade Deck

DRESS FOR THE EVENING: Casual
Remember to please have your luggage outside your cabin door between 6:00 PM & 1:00 AM!
Movie "Running Scared": 7:30, 10:00, 12:30, 3:00, 5:30, 8:00, 10:30 and 1:00 AM.

THANK YOU FOR CRUISING ON THE "JUBILEE"! HAVE A SAFE TRIP HOME!

Today aboard the Starcruise

There's Magic Aboard.

PREMIER CRUISE LINES

Kid's Call!

Special Activities for kids ages 2 to 7.

Your Captain:
D. KONTZANIKOLAOU

Your Starcruise Director:
JIM WARD

Schedule of Activities
Onboard Premier Starships
KIDS CLUB HOUSE
PREMIER DECK AFT

MONDAY

The Kids Club House is open from 6 p.m. until 1 a.m.
Babysitting: 10 p.m. until 1 a.m.

* Scheduled Activities

TIME	ACTIVITIES	LOCATION
2:00	MUSIC & MUNCHIES	SATELLITE CAFE
4:00	**SAY "HELLO" TO YOUR STARCRUISE DIRECTOR, JIM WARD, AND YOUR "OCEANIC" YOUTH STAFF.**	BROADWAY SHOWROOM
4:10 - 4:30	★ JOIN SAMANTHA, LOUISE, KICKI, PAULA, NICOLA, MARCIA, ALISSON, KATHERINE, ROBIN, SUE AND DENISE FOR A PARTY WITH YOUR DISNEY FRIENDS. WE WILL PARADE FROM THE BROADWAY SHOWROOM UP TO THE KIDS ROOM. SO COME ALONG AND JOIN US AS WE SAIL OUT ON OUR FUN-FILLED CRUISE TO THE BAHAMAS. ★	KIDS CLUB HOUSE PREMIER DECK
6:00	MAIN SEATING DINNER IS SERVED - THE ITALIAN WAY! MAGNIFICO!!	SEVEN CONTINENTS DINING ROOM
5:30	**PARENTS PLEASE ATTEND AN ORIENTATION TALK GIVEN BY YOUTH DIRECTOR, SAMANTHA. AT THIS TIME THE PROGRAM WILL BE DISCUSSED AS WELL AS BABY-SITTING SERVICES! THANK YOU!! MEET IN THE BROAD-WAY SHOWROOM.**	**BROADWAY SHOWROOM LOUNGE DECK FWD.**
6:00 - 10:00	★ COME ALONG AND REGISTER AT THE KID'S ROOM	★ KIDS CLUB HOUSE PREMIER DECK
7:00 - 7:45	★ LET'S START THE FUN WITH A COLORING COMPETITION. HOW IMAGINATIVE ARE YOU ALL? CAN YOU DRAW A SPRING PICTURE?	
7:45 - 8:45	DO YOU KNOW HOW TO PLAY THE NAME GAME, DOGGIE DOGGIE, HEADS UP SEVEN UP? WE HAVE SO MANY GAMES TO PLAY. WE WILL EVEN TEACH YOU THE CAPTAIN'S FAVORITE GAME.	
8:45 - 9:30	IN ARTS AND CRAFTS TONIGHT WE WILL MAKE OCEANIC SHIP SOUVENIRS.	
9:30 - 10:00	AS WE START TO YAWN AND GROW SLEEPY, LET'S CURL UP AND LISTEN TO A GOODNIGHT STORY.	
8:15	LATE SEATING DINNER IS SERVED - THE ITALIAN WAY! MAGNIFICO!!	SEVEN CONTINENTS DINING ROOM
10:00	MOVIETIME (SEE SCHEDULE)	HOLLYWOOD THEATER

Today aboard the Starcruise

There's Magic Aboard.

PREMIER CRUISE LINES

Kids Call

Special Activities for kids ages 2 to 7.

Your Captain:
D. KONTZANIKOLAOU

Your Starcruise Director: The Kids Club House is open from 8:30 a.m. until 1:30 a.m.
JIM WARD   Babysitting: 10 p.m. until 1:30 a.m.
*Scheduled Activities

TUESDAY

TIME	ACTIVITIES	LOCATION
	★★★★★★★★★★★★★★★★★★★★★★★★★★★★★★★★	
8:30 - 9:15*	★"CARTOON TIME." SEE MICKEY, MINNIE, DONALD AND PLUTO ★ WITH THEIR FRIENDS IN ACTION!	KIDS CLUB HOUSE PREMIER DECK
9:15 - 9:45*	★ TOUR THE S.S. OCEANIC'S BRIDGE FROM STEM TO STERN AND ★ GET YOUR PHOTO TAKEN WHEN YOU STEER THE SHIP!	**PARENTS PLEASE NOTE: WE LEAVE PROMPTLY AT 9:15**
9:45 - 10:15*	★"GOOFYCISE". GO GOOFY AND WILD AND BECOME A FIT ★ CHILD!!	
	★★★★★★★★★★★★★★★★★★★★★★★★★★★★★★★★★★	

★★★

10:15 - 11:15*	**NOW IT'S TIME FOR THE HIGHLIGHT OF THE MORNING!!! IT'S PARTY TIME!!!**	
	PREMIER PRESENTS DOUG THE MAGICIAN	LET'S WATCH OUR AMAZING MAGICIAN "DOUG", AS HE MYSTERIOUSLY SURPRISES US WITH HIS MAGIC TRICKS. CAN YOU TELL HOW HE DOES THEM? DO YOU KNOW THE MAGIC WORDS TO FIND OUR DISNEY FRIENDS? MAYBE DOUG CAN HELP! LET'S CELEBRATE AT OUR VERY OWN WALT DISNEY UNBIRTHDAY PARTY!	STARLIGHT CABARET LOUNGE DECK

★★★

TIME	ACTIVITIES	LOCATION
	★★★★★★★★★★★★★★★★★★★★★★★★★★★★★★★★★	
11:15 - 12:00*	★LET'S ALL GO SWIMMING IN OUR "SPLASH POOL" OR MAYBE ★ PLAY ON THE CLIMBING FRAME OR ROCKING HORSE IN OUR ★ PLAYGROUND.	KIDS CLUB HOUSE PREMIER DECK
	★★★★★★★★★★★★★★★★★★★★★★★★★★★★★★★★★	
11:15	HORSE RACING - PICK A PONY	RIVIERA POOLS-POOL DECK
12:00	LUNCH TIME!!	
12:00	THE S.S. OCEANIC SAILS INTO PRINCE GEORGE HARBOR	
12:30	WELCOME TO NASSAU, BAHAMAS!!	
12:00 - 7:00	THE KID'S ROOM IS OPEN FOR YOU TO PLAY, DRAW A PICTURE OR PERHAPS WATCH A FILM WHILE DOING A PUZZLE WITH YOUR "OCEANIC" COUNSELORS YOU'LL ALWAYS RETURN FOR MORE!	KIDS CLUB HOUSE PREMIER DECK
4:30	AN AFTERNOON CARTOON MOVIE	HOLLYWOOD THEATER
5:00 & 7:00	JOIN IN THE FUN FOR THE CAPTAIN'S PARTY AND MEET THE CAPTAIN AND HIS SENIOR OFFICERS!	BROADWAY SHOWROOM

Today aboard the Starcruise

PREMIER CRUISE LINES

There's Magic Aboard.

Kids Call

Special Activities for kids ages 2 to 7.

Your Captain:
D. KONTZANIKOLAOU

WELCOME TO SALT CAY ISLAND

Your Starcruise Director:
JIM WARD

The Kids Club House is open from 1 p.m. until 1 a.m.
Babysitting: 10 p.m. until 1 a.m.

WEDNESDAY

*Scheduled Activities

TIME	ACTIVITIES	LOCATION
6:00	STARSHIP OCEANIC SAILS FOR SALT CAY	
8:00	**"BEWARE OF PIRATES"** - STARSHIP OCEANIC DROPS ANCHOR OFF SALT CAY	

★★★★★★★★★★★★★★★★★★★★★★★★★★★★★★★★★
★ AS SOON AS THE FIRST TENDER HAS ARRIVED WE GO ★
★ STRAIGHT INTO OUR BEACH ACTIVITIES! SO LISTEN OUT FOR ★
★ OUR ANNOUNCEMENTS. WE WILL BE DOWN ON THE BEACH, ★
★ CLOSE TO THE PAVILLION. ★
★ MAYBE WE WILL FIND BURIED TREASURE THERE! OR MAYBE ★
★ WE MIGHT BURY A COUNSELOR IN THE SAND!! AND WHO CAN ★
★ BUILD THE BEST SAND CASTLE OR SCULPTURE!! ★
★★★★★★★★★★★★★★★★★★★★★★★★★★★★★★★★★
★ FOR PARENTS WISHING TO LEAVE THEIR CHILDREN FOR ★
★ BEACH SUPERVISION, COUNSELORS WILL BE ON DUTY DOWN ★
★ ON THE BEACH CLOSE TO THE PAVILLION, AFTER THE ★
★ ARRIVAL OF THE EARLY BIRD TENDER STRAIGHT THROUGH ★
★ UNTIL 30 MINUTES BEFORE THE LAST TENDER LEAVES. ★
★ UNFORTUNATELY WE ARE UNABLE TO TAKE THE CHILDREN ★
★ SWIMMING. ★
★★★★★★★★★★★★★★★★★★★★★★★★★★★★★★★★★

TIME	ACTIVITIES	LOCATION
11:30 - 1:30	LUNCH TIME - BUCANEER BURGERS	
	– BACK ON THE SHIP –	
2:00 - 5:00	BUILD A SUNDAE	ICE CREAM PARLOR- POOL DECK

★★★★★★★★★★★★★★★★★★★★★★★★★★★★★★★★★
★ THE KIDS ROOM IS OPEN FOR YOU TO PLAY, MAYBE YOU ★
★ WOULD LIKE TO WATCH AN AFTERNOON MOVIE OR PERHAPS ★
★ PLAY WITH OUR GAMES AND TOYS. ★
★★★★★★★★★★★★★★★★★★★★★★★★★★★★★★★★★

TIME	ACTIVITIES	LOCATION
1:00 - 7:00	THE KIDS ROOM IS OPEN	KIDS CLUB HOUSE
4:30	AN AFTERNOON CARTOON MOVIE	HOLLYWOOD THEATER

Today aboard the Starcruise

There's Magic Aboard.

PREMIER CRUISE LINES

Kid's Call   Special Activities for kids ages 2 to 7.

Your Captain:
D. KONTZANIKOLAOU

Your Starcruise Director: The Kids Club House is open from 9 a.m.-12 p.m., 1:45 p.m.-5 p.m.   **THURSDAY**
JIM WARD   (3:20 until 4 p.m., closed for the masquerade), 6-1 a.m.
* Scheduled Activities   Babysitting: 10 p.m. until 1 a.m.

TIME	ACTIVITIES	LOCATION
9:00 - 9:45*	"IT'S CARTOON TIME" - LET'S ALL SAY GOODBYE TO MICKEY, MINNIE AND DONALD AND PLUTO!	KIDS CLUB HOUSE PREMIER DECK
9:45 - 10:15*	"BALLOON MESSAGES!!" SEND A MESSAGE TO A FARAWAY LAND. IT WILL WASH ASHORE AND LAND IN THE SAND! PERHAPS AN ANSWER FROM A NEW FOUND FRIEND... WAIT FOR A REPLY THEY MAY SEND!!!	
10:15 - 10:45*	COME ALONG FOR A MORNING FULL OF FUN WITH AN EXERCISE CLASS GIVEN BY YOUR CRAZY FUN COUNSELORS.	
10:45 - 11:15	PAINTING TIME! CREATE A MASTERPIECE, SEE WHAT YOU CAN DO!	KIDS CALL CLUB HOUSE PREMIER DECK
11:15 - 12:00*	"IT'S SPLASHPOOL TIME" AFTER A MORNING OF ARTS N' CRAFTS, JOIN US IN THE SPLASHPOOL FOR SOME LAUGHS! LET'S PLAY SOME WATERGAMES AS WE SAIL, IT'S BEACH TIME, LET'S PLAY WITH SPADE AND PAILS!	
11:15	TALENT SHOW REGISTRATION	STARLIGHT CABARET
12:00 - 2:00	LUNCHTIME	
1:30 - 3:00	MASQUERADE SUPPLIES ARE AVAILABLE!! PARENTS COME ALONG AND HELP MAKE YOUR CHILD'S MASQUERADE COSTUME!! THERE'S PLENTY OF IDEAS, MICKEY, MINNIE, AN INDIAN, A PIRATE, M & M'S, A FLOWER, A PRINCESS, A BUTTERFLY OR COME UP WITH YOUR OWN IDEA!	LOUNGE DECK FORWARD
2:00	MOVIETIME (SEE MOVIE SCHEDULE)	HOLLYWOOD THEATER
2:00 - 5:00	BUILD A SUNDAE	POOL DECK

Starcruiser

Special Activities for special passengers ages 8 to 12.

Schedule of Activities
Onboard Premier's Starships

SPACE STATION
POOL DECK AFT

MONDAY

Your Captain: D. KONTZANIKOLAOU
Your Starcruise Director: JIM WARD

*SUPERVISED

TIME	ACTIVITIES	LOCATION
2:00	MUSIC & MUNCHES	SATELLITE CAFE
4:00	COME MEET YOUR STARCRUISE DIRECTOR JIM WARD AND MEET YOUR YOUTH STAFF.	BROADWAY SHOWROOM
	★★ JOIN SAMANTHA, LOUISE, KICKI, PAULA, NICOLA, MARCIA, ALISSON, KATHERINE, ROBIN, SUE AND DENISE FOR A PARTY WITH YOUR DISNEY FRIENDS. WE WILL PARADE FROM THE BROADWAY SHOWROOM UP TO THE KIDS ROOM. SO COME ALONG AND JOIN US AS WE SAIL OUT ON OUR FUN-FILLED CRUISE TO THE BAHAMAS. ★★	KIDS CLUB HOUSE PREMIER DECK
4:10 - 4:30		
4:45	"BUCKLE UP BOATDRILL": LEARN THE SAFETY RULES OF THE S.S. OCEANIC	
6:00	MAIN SEATING DINNER - ITALIAN NIGHT - MAGNIFICO!	SEVEN CONTINENTS
6:00 - 10:00*	WELCOME ABOARD! COME ALONG AND MEET YOUR COUNSELORS AND REGISTER FOR YOUR ACTIVITIES THROUGHOUT THE CRUISE. LET'S BEGIN OUR EVENING AND MAKE NEW FRIENDS PLAYING BOARD GAMES LIKE MONOPOLY, CLUE, SCRABBLE, CONNECT FOUR, OPERATION, RISK, STRATEGO AND MANY MORE!!! TO CONTINUE OUR EVENING OF FUN LET'S PLAY GAMES SUCH AS THE NAME GAME, FOUR CORNERS, FREEZE, HOT POTATO, PASS THE PARCEL, HEADS-UP SEVEN-UP ..... NOW WE ARE HAVING FUN! LET'S HAVE A DISCO AND GET SOME PRACTICE FOR OUR DISCO DANCING COMPETITION TO BE HELD LATER ON IN THE CRUISE! BEFORE YOU LEAVE FOR THE NIGHT, **DON'T FORGET TO PICK UP YOUR AUTOGRAPH HUNT!** DON'T FORGET THEY MUST BE HANDED IN THE LAST NIGHT OF YOUR CRUISE BEFORE 8 P.M.!! SO GO AND HUNT DOWN THOSE OFFICERS, STAFF AND CREW!!!	SPACE STATION CENTER

Starcruiser

Special Activities for special passengers ages 8 to 12.

SPACE STATION
POOL DECK AFT

TUESDAY

Your Captain: D. KONTZANIKOLAOU
Your Starcruise Director: JIM WARD

*SUPERVISED

TIME	ACTIVITIES	LOCATION
9:00 - 12:00*	CARTOON TIME. SEE MICKEY, DONALD AND GOOFY WITH THEIR FRIENDS IN ACTION.	SPACE STATION CENTER
9:00 - 9:30	THE CAPTAIN AND HIS OFFICERS INVITE YOU TO TOUR THE BRIDGE OF THE S/S OCEANIC AND LET OUR PHOTOGRAPHERS	
9:45 - 10:15	TAKE YOUR PICTURE WHILE YOU STEER THE SHIP.	
	★★ NOW IT'S TIME FOR THE HIGHLIGHT OF THE MORNING!!! IT'S PARTY TIME!!! ★★	STARLIGHT CABARET LOUNGE DECK
10:15 - 11:15*	LET'S WATCH OUR AMAZING MAGICIAN "DOUG", AS HE MYSTERIOUSLY SURPRISES US WITH HIS MAGIC TRICKS. CAN YOU TELL HOW HE DOES THEM? DO YOU KNOW THE MAGIC WORDS TO FIND OUR DISNEY FRIENDS? MAYBE DOUG CAN HELP! LET'S CELEBRATE AT OUR VERY OWN WALT DISNEY UNBIRTHDAY PARTY!	
11:15 - 12:00*	POOL GAMES - SPLASH AND SWIM WITH YOUR FRIENDS AND MAYBE PLAY MARCO POLO OR HAVE YOU GOT A NEW GAME?	POOL SIDE
11:30	HORSE RACING - PICK A PONY	
12:00	THE S/S OCEANIC SAILS INTO PRINCE GEORGE HARBOR	RIVIERA POOLS
12:00 - 2:00	LUNCH IS SERVED	
2:00 - 5:00	THE ICE CREAM PARLOR IS OPEN TO BUILD YOUR OWN SUNDAE	BIG DIPPER ICE CREAM PARLOR
4:00	MOVIETIME - (SEE MOVIE SCHEDULE)	HOLLYWOOD THEATER
5:00 & 7:00	KIDS, JOIN YOUR PARENTS AT THE CAPTAIN'S COCKTAIL PARTY, WHERE YOU'LL MEET CAPTAIN CHILAS AND HIS OFFICERS.	BROADWAY SHOWROOM
6:00	DINNER IS SERVED - THE FRENCH WAY - OOH LA LA!!	SEVEN CONTINENTS RESTAURANT
6:00 - 10:00	★★ TONIGHT'S THE NIGHT TO WIN PRIZES. ARE YOU A BUDDING ARTIST? CAN YOU WIN OUR DRAWING COMPETITION? COME ALONG AND COLOR YOUR BEST PICTURE. IT'S BINGO TIME! LISTEN FOR THE NUMBERS AND DON'T FORGET TO SHOUT! HOW MUCH DO YOU KNOW ABOUT WALT DISNEY? TEST YOUR KNOWLEDGE IN DISNEY TRIVIA! AND TO END OUR EVENING OF FUN WE SHALL PLAY SOME CRAZY MUSIC GAMES. THIS IS THE LAST CHANCE TO PRACTICE FOR THE DANCING COMPETITION! ★★	SPACE STATION CENTER

Special Activities for special passengers ages 8 to 12.

Your Captain:
D. KONTZANIKOLAOU
Your Starcruise Director:
JIM WARD
*SUPERVISED

WELCOME TO SALT CAY ISLAND   **WEDNESDAY**

TIME	ACTIVITIES	LOCATION
6:00	STARSHIP OCEANIC SAILS FOR SALT CAY	
8:00	STARSHIP OCEANIC DROPS ANCHOR OFF SALT CAY	

★★★
★ AS SOON AS THE FIRST TENDER HAS ARRIVED WE GO ★
★ STRAIGHT INTO OUR BEACH ACTIVITIES! SO LISTEN OUT FOR ★
★ OUR ANNOUNCEMENTS. WE WILL BE DOWN ON THE BEACH, ★
★ CLOSE TO THE PAVILLION. ★
★ MAYBE WE WILL FIND BURIED TREASURE THERE! OR MAYBE ★
★ WE MIGHT BURY A COUNSELOR IN THE SAND!! WE WILL ALSO ★
★ DISCOVER WHO CAN BUILD THE BEST SAND CASTLE OR ★
★ SCULPTURE!! ★
★ MAYBE YOU WILL EVEN TAKE PART IN THE "SPLASH DOWN" ★
★ PROGRAM OFFERED BY THE DIVERS. ★
★★★
★ FOR PARENTS WISHING TO LEAVE THEIR CHILDREN FOR ★
★ BEACH SUPERVISION, COUNSELORS WILL BE ON DUTY DOWN ★
★ ON THE BEACH CLOSE TO THE PAVILLION, AFTER THE ★
★ ARRIVAL OF THE EARLY BIRD TENDER STRAIGHT THROUGH ★
★ UNTIL 30 MINUTES BEFORE THE LAST TENDER LEAVES. ★
★ UNFORTUNATELY WE ARE UNABLE TO TAKE THE CHILDREN ★
★ SWIMMING. ★
★★★

TIME	ACTIVITIES	LOCATION
11:30 - 1:30	LUNCHTIME - BUCANEER BURGER	
	– BACK ON THE SHIP –	
2:00 - 5:00	BUILD A SUNDAE	ICE CREAM PARLOR - POOL DECK
5:30	S.S. OCEANIC HEADS FOR PORT CANAVERAL	
6:00	MAIN SEATING DINNER - CARIBBEAN DELIGHTS	SEVEN CONTINENTS DINING ROOM
8:15	LATE SEATING DINNER - CARIBBEAN DELIGHTS	SEVEN CONTINENTS DINING ROOM

★★★★★★★★★★★★★★★★★★★★★★★★★★★★★★★★★★★★★★
6:00 - 10:00* ★ BRING ALONG THOSE AUTOGRAPH HUNTS ... DO YOU HAVE ★   SPACE STATION CENTER
★ ANYTHING UNUSUAL WITH YOU OR SOMETHING YOU LIKE A ★
★ LOT? BRING IT ALONG FOR SHOW AND TELL ... THEN, JUST ★
★ LIKE THE "REAL THING" WE'LL TURN THE SPACE STATION ★
★ CENTER INTO A MOVIE THEATER WITH POPCORN AND SODA ★
★ AND WATCH A FAVORITE MOVIE. ★
★★★★★★★★★★★★★★★★★★★★★★★★★★★★★★★★★★★★★★

TIME	ACTIVITIES	LOCATION
10:00	MOVIETIME (SEE SCHEDULE)	HOLLYWOOD THEATER
12:00	MIDNIGHT BUFFET	SEVEN CONTINENTS DINING ROOM

Starcruiser

Special Activities for special passengers ages 8 to 12.

Your Captain:
D. KONTZANIKOLAOU

Your Starcruise Director:
JIM WARD

SPACE STATION
POOL DECK AFT

THURSDAY

TIME	ACTIVITIES	LOCATION
9:00 - 9:30	★★★★★★★★★★★★★★★★★★★★★★★★★★★★★★★★★ ★ MORNING CARTOONS. COME WATCH MICKEY AND MINNIE ★ ★ WITH THEIR FRIENDS.	SPACE STATION CENTER
9:30 - 10:15	★ "SCAVENGER HUNT". GET A LIST, GET ON A TEAM, KEEP ★ ★ TOGETHER, COLLECT ALL THE ITEMS AND WIN A PRIZE. ★	SPACE STATION CENTER
10:15 - 10:45	★ COME ALONG FOR A MORNING FULL OF FUN WITH YOUR ★ ★ COUNSELORS. COME JOIN US FOR DISNEYCISE, AN EXERCISE ★ ★ CLASS GIVEN BY YOUR CRAZY FUN FRIENDS.	SPACE STATION
11:00 - 11:15 11:00 - 12:00	★ RIDDLE TIME. CAN YOU GUESS THE RIDDLE? ★ ★ CHOOSE YOUR CAPTAINS AND JOIN A TEAM FOR POOL ★ ★ OLYMPICS.	SPACE STATION CENTER TEEN CENTER
	★ "JR. POOL OLYMPICS" - DIVE IN FOR AN OBJECT. RACE YOUR ★ ★ WAY TO VICTORY. ★★★★★★★★★★★★★★★★★★★★★★★★★★★★★★★★★	POOLSIDE
12:00 - 2:00	LUNCHTIME	
11:15	TALENT SHOW REGISTRATION	STARLIGHT CABARET
12:00 - 2:00	LUNCHTIME	
2:00 - 5:00	BUILD A SUNDAE	ICE CREAM PARLOR - POOL DECK
1:30 - 3:00	★★★★★★★★★★★★★★★★★★★★★★★★★★★★★★★★★ ★ MASQUERADE SUPPLIES ARE AVAILABLE. COME ALONG AND ★ ★ PICK UP YOUR SUPPLIES: POSTERBOARD, CREPE PAPER, ★ ★ RIBBONS AND BALLOONS TO MAKE YOUR COSTUME. ARE YOU ★ ★ GOING TO BE A PIRATE, AN M & M, HERSHEY'S KISS OR A ★ ★ CLOWN OR THINK UP ONE OF YOUR OWN. ★★★★★★★★★★★★★★★★★★★★★★★★★★★★★★★★★	**LOUNGE DECK FWD.**
3:00 - 3:15	★ NOTE TO PARENTS: REGISTRATION FOR THE PARADE TAKES ★ ★ PLACE IN THE KID'S CLUB HOUSE! THE PARADE WILL PRO- ★ ★ CEED TO THE BROADWAY SHOWROOM, LOUNGE DECK. ★★★★★★★★★★★★★★★★★★★★★★★★★★★★★★★★★	KID'S CLUB HOUSE
3:30 - 4:00	**THE GRAND MASQUERADE!** WHO ARE OUR SPECIAL JUDGES?	BROADWAY SHOWROOM LOUNGE DECK FORWARD
4:15 - 5:00*	★★★★★★★★★★★★★★★★★★★★★★★★★★★★★★★★★ ★ "ICE CREAM PARTY" AFTER THE PARADE, AND A FINE JOB YOU ★ ★ DID, LET'S JOIN IN FOR ICE CREAM WITH THE OTHER KIDS! ★ ★ JOIN MICKEY AND FRIENDS FOR CARTOON FUN, AS THE S.S. ★ ★ OCEANIC SAILS INTO THE SETTING SUN! ★★★★★★★★★★★★★★★★★★★★★★★★★★★★★★★★★	KID'S CLUB HOUSE
5:00	S.S. OCEANIC TALENT SHOW	BROADWAY SHOWROOM
6:00	MAIN SEATING DINNER - AMERICA THE BEAUTIFUL	SEVEN CONTINENTS DINING ROOM
8:15	LATE SEATING DINNER - AMERICA THE BEAUTIFUL	SEVEN CONTINENTS DINING ROOM

5 Cruise Guides to Help
Plan Your Cruise Vacation

Here are 5 Cruise Guides to help you plan your next cruise. The Cruise Guides are produced by Cruise Lines International Association (CLIA).

* Worldwide Cruise Destination Guide
* Cruise Guide For Active Adults
* Cruise Guide For the Wheelchair Traveler
* Cruise Guide For Honeymooners
* Cruise Guide for Children

CLIA is one of the largest and most influential travel industry associations. CLIA has 34 member cruise lines and over 19,000 travel agency affiliates.

CLIA's training programs allow professional travel agents to stay on top of the constantly changing cruise ship market. Look for the CLIA logo when you book your next cruise vacation.

FREE!
"Cruising: Answers to your most asked questions" Free 20 page pamphlet . CLIA, 500 Fifth Ave. Suite 1407, New York, N.Y.10110 Send self-addressed stamped envelope (45 cents postage)

Cruise
Lines
International
Association

The World's Leading
Cruise Lines and Travel Agents
Working Together

WORLDWIDE CRUISE DESTINATION GUIDE

Destination	Abercrombie Cruises	Alaska Pacific Cruises	American Hawaii Cruises	Bermuda Star Line	Carnival Cruise Lines	Chandris Fantasy Cruises	Clipper Cruise Line	Commodore Cruise Line	Costa Cruises	Crown Cruise Line	Crystal Cruises	Cunard Line	CunardNAC	Cunard Sea Goddess	Delta Queen Steamboat Co.	Dolphin Cruise Line	Dolphin Hellas Cruises	Epirotiki Lines	Holland America Line	Norwegian Cruise Line	Ocean Cruise Line	Pearl Cruises	Premier Cruise Lines	Princess Cruises	Regency Cruises	Renaissance Cruises/Sitmar Cruises	Royal Caribbean Cruise Line	Royal Cruise Line	Royal Viking Line	Seabourn Cruise Line	Sea Venture Cruises	Society Expeditions Cruises	Sun Line Cruises	Windstar Sail Cruises	World Explorer Cruises
Alaska	•		•		•		•	•				•				•		•	•	•				•	•		•	•	•	•			•		•
Antarctica						•																										•			
Australia	•					•						•						•				•		•					•	•					
Bahamas				•	•			•								•							•				•								
Bermuda				•	•							•								•				•			•			•					
British Isles												•						•						•					•	•					
Canada-West		•																																	
Canada/New England					•		•					•						•						•				•		•					
Canadian Arctic																																			
Canary Islands																		•																	
Caribbean				•	•	•	•	•	•	•	•	•				•		•	•	•			•	•	•	•	•	•	•	•			•	•	
Cruise to Nowhere				•	•	•				•						•																			
East Coast					•	•																													
Galapagos Islands																																•			
Greenland																																			
Hawaii	•	•																•		•				•				•							
Indonesia/Southeast Asia																						•							•			•			
Mediterranean					•				•		•	•	•			•		•	•	•				•	•	•	•	•	•	•			•	•	
Mexico	•				•	•			•	•	•	•				•		•	•	•				•	•		•	•		•					
Orient										•	•	•						•				•		•	•			•						•	
Pacific										•				•																					
River – U.S.															•																				
River – South America					•											•		•									•		•			•			
Russia/Europe											•																•		•						
Scandinavia											•													•			•		•						
South America			•		•											•		•									•		•			•			
Tahiti																		•										•							
Trans-Atlantic				•					•		•	•							•					•				•	•	•			•		
Trans-Pacific				•					•		•	•				•								•				•	•				•		
Trans-Panama					•						•	•						•						•				•	•				•		
World												•																	•						•

Cruise Guide For Active Adults

	Admiral Cruises	Aloha Pacific Cruises	American Hawaii Cruises	Bermuda Star Line	Carnival Cruise Line	Chandris Fantasy Cruises	Clipper Cruise Line	Commodore Cruise Line	Costa Cruises	Crown Cruise Line	Crystal Cruises	Cunard Line	Cunard/NAC	Cunard Sea Goddess	Cunard Steamboat Co.	Delta Queen Steamboat Co.	Dolphin Cruise Line	Dolphin Hellas Cruises	Epirotiki Lines	Holland America Line	Norwegian Cruise Line	Ocean Cruise Lines	Pearl Cruises of Scandinavia	Premier Cruise Line	Princess Cruises	Regency Cruises	Royal Cruise Line(Slimar Cruises)	Royal Caribbean Cruise Line	Royal Viking Line	Seabourn Cruise Line	Sea Venture Cruises	Societe Expeditions Cruises	Sun Line Cruises	Windstar Sail Cruises	World Explorer Cruises
ON-BOARD																																			
Aerobics	A	A	A	A	A	A		A	A	A	A	A	A		S	A	A	S	A	A	A	A	A	A	A	A	A	A	A	A	A	S	S		A
Basketball					A	S			S				S							S				A		S	A	S	A						
Low Cal Menu Choices	A	A	A		A	A	A	A	A		A	S	A	A		A		A		A	A	A	A	A	A	A	A	A	A		A		A		A
Golf Driving			S	S	A	S		A	S	A		A	A							S	S		A	A	S	S	A	S	A						
Gym	S		S	S	A	A		A	A		A	A	A	A	S	S	S	S	A	A	A	A	A	A	A	A	A	S	A	A	A	A	A	S	A
Jogging	S	A	A	A	A	A			A		A	A	A	A		A	A	S	A	A	A	S	A	A	A	S	A	A	A	A	A	S	A		A
Masseuse	S	A	A		A	A		A	A	A	A	A	A	A	S		S	S	A	A	A	A	A	A	A	S	S	A	A	A	A	S	S	A	A
Paddle Tennis	A	A	A		A	A		A		A	A			A		A	S	A		S		A		A		A		A					S		A
Sail Boating			A			S															A								A					A/SP	
Sauna	S	A	A		A	A			A	S	A	A	A	A	S		S	S	A	A	A	A		A	A	S	A	A	A	A	A	S	A		A
Scuba Diving	S				S	S	S	A	S																		A				A		A/SP		
Skeet/Trap Shooting	A			A	A	A		A	A	A	A						A	S	A	A	A	A	A	A	A	A	A	A	A		A	A	A	A	
Snorkeling	S			S	A	S		S					A/SP		A						A				A					A	A	A	S	A/SP	
Snorkeling Lessons	S		A	S		S	S	A	S					A						A			A			A	A	A			A	A	A		
Spa Pool	S				S				S	S		A	A	A	S	S	S	S	S		A	A	S	A	S	A	S	S	A	A	A				
Swimming	A	A	A	A	A	A		A	A	A	A	A	A	A	A	A	A	A	A	A	A	A	A	A	A	A	A	A	A	S	A	A	S	A	A
Total Fitness Program	S	A	A						S			A	A	A			S	A	A	A	A	A	A	A	A	A	S	A	A		S				
Volleyball				S	S						A	S					S			A	S	S		S	A									S	
Water Skiing				S									A/SP																A				A/SP	
Windsurfing				S									A/SP															A			S		A/SP	
ASHORE*																																			
Bicycling		A	A		A/I	A/I	I	A		A	A	A	A				A/I		I			I	A	I	I	I	A		A	I	A/I	S	I		
Charter Fishing	S	A	A		A/I	S	I	A	S	S	A	A	A	A			A/I	A	I			S	A	I	I	A		A	I	A/I	S	A			
Golf	A	A	A	S	A	S	A	A	S	S	A	A	A		A/I	A	A	S	I	I		A	I	A	A	A	A	I	A/I	S	I			
Hiking		A			A/I	A/I	I	A	S		A	A	A	A		A/I		I		I	A	I	I	I	A		A	I	A/I	I				
Horseback Riding	S	A	A		A	A/I	I	A	S		A	A	A	A		A/I		I		I	A	I	I	I	A		A	I	A/I	S				
Scuba Diving	S	A	A	S	A	S	S	A	S	S	A	A	A		A/I	A	A		I		A	A		I	A		A	A	A/I	A				
Snorkeling	S	A	A	A	A	S	A	A	S	S	A	A	A	A	A/I	A	A	S	S	A	A	S	A	I	A		A	A	A/I	A				
Tennis	A	A	A		A/I	S	I	A	S	S	A	A	A	A		A/I	A	S			I	A	I	I	A	A	A	I	A/I	I	A	I		
Water Skiing			A		A/I	S	I	A	S	S	A	A	A		A/I	A	I		I	A	I	I	I	A		A	S	A/I	A					
Windsurfing		A	A		A/I	S	I	A	S	S	A	A	A		A/I	A	I		I	A	I	I	I	A		A	S	A/I	A					

EXPLANATION KEY

A: All Ships
S: Some Ships
SP: Ship(s) equipped with aft water sports platform
I: Information on local facilities provided by shipboard staff.

*NOTE:

(1) There is an additional charge for most shore-side activities. Some shipboard activities, such as skeet shooting, are also extra.

(2) Some water and shore-side sports aren't available in every port or destination (i.e., snorkeling in Alaska).

(3) Unless marked "I," available shore-side activities are provided through shore excursions and sports programs OR arranged at a passenger's request.

Cruise Guide for the Wheelchair Traveler

VESSELS	Access wheelchair pages	Passengers must be accompanied	Accept regular wheelchairs	Narrow fit–wide wheelchairs	Wide doors	Elevators – Lowering lifts	CABINS – Bath with rails	CABINS – Ramps available	Public Rooms – Ramps available	Public Rooms – Access to all public rooms	DECKS – Access to all passenger areas
Aegean Dolphin	X	X		X						X	
Amerikanis	X	X		X						X	
Atlantic	X	X	X		X	X	X			X	X
Azur	X	X		X						X	
Azure Sea	X	X		X							
Bermuda Star	X	X	X		X	X			X	X	
Britanis	X	X		X						X	
Caribe I	X	X		X	X						
Carla Costa	X	X	X		X				X	X	
Carnivale	X	X		X					X	X	
Celebration	X	X		X	X	X	X	X	X	X	X
Constitution	X	X	X		X				X	X	
Costa Riviera	X	X	X		X				X	X	
Crown Del Mar	X	X		X			X			X	X
Crown Odyssey	X	X	X		X	X	X	X	X	X	X
Cunard Countess	X	X	X							X	
Cunard Princess	X	X	X							X	
Danae	X	X		X	X					X	X
Daphne	X	X		X	X	X				X	X
Dawn Princess	X	X	X						X	X	
Dolphin	X	X		X						X	
Emerald Seas	X	X		X	X	X				X	X
Enrico Costa	X	X		X						X	
Eugenio Costa	X	X		X						X	
Fair Princess	X	X	X						X		X
Festivale	X	X		X						X	
Galileo	X	X		X						X	
Golden Odyssey	X	X		X					X	X	X
Holiday	X	X		X	X	X	X	X	X	X	X
Independence	X	X	X		X				X		X
Ionian Dolphin	X										
Island Princess	X	X	X		X	X	X		X	X	
Jubilee	X	X		X	X	X	X	X	X	X	X
Mardi Gras	X	X		X					X	X	
Mississippi Queen	X	X	X						X	X	
Nantucket Clipper	X	X								X	
Newport Clipper	X	X								X	
Nieuw Amsterdam	X	X	X		X	X	X	X	X	X	X
Noordam	X	X	X		X	X	X	X	X	X	X
Nordic Prince	X		X							X	
Norway	X		X	X	X				X		X
Ocean Islander	X	X		X			X			X	X
Ocean Pearl	X	X	X		X	X			X		X
Ocean Princess	X	X		X			X			X	X
Pacific Princess	X	X	X		X	X	X		X	X	
Queen of Bermuda	X	X	X				X			X	X
Queen Elizabeth 2	X	X	X		X	X	X	X	X	X	X
Regent Sea	X	X	X	X	X	X	X		X	X	X

VESSELS	Access wheelchair pages	Passengers must be accompanied	Accept regular wheelchairs	Narrow fit–wide wheelchairs	Wide doors	Elevators – Lowering lifts	CABINS – Bath with rails	CABINS – Ramps available	Public Rooms – Ramps available	Public Rooms – Access to all public rooms	DECKS – Access to all passenger areas
Regent Star	X	X	X	X	X			X	X	X	X
Regent Sun	X	X	X		X				X		X
Romanza	X	X	X		X				X		
Rotterdam	X	X	X	X	X	X	X	X	X	X	X
Royal Princess	X	X	X		X	X	X	X	X	X	X
Royal Viking Sea	X	X		X	X	X	X	X	X	X	X
Royal Viking Sky	X	X		X	X	X	X	X	X	X	X
Royal Viking Star	X	X		X	X	X	X	X	X	X	X
Royal Viking Sun	X	X		X	X	X	X	X	X	X	X
Sagafjord	X	X		X		X	X	X	X	X	X
Seabourn Pride	X	X	X		X			X	X	X	X
Sea Breeze	X	X		X						X	
Sea Goddess I	X	X	X						X	X	
Sea Goddess II	X	X	X						X	X	
Sea Princess	X	X	X		X					X	
Sea Venture	X	X	X		X					X	
Seaward	X	X		X	X	X	X			X	X
Sky Princess	X	X	X		X	X			X	X	X
Skyward	X	X	X		X	X				X	
Song of America	X	X		X						X	
Song of Norway	X	X		X							
Southward	X	X		X						X	
Sovereign of the Seas	X	X		X					X	X	X
Stardancer	X	X		X	X	X	X	X	X	X	X
Star/Ship Atlantic	X	X		X				X			
Star/Ship Oceanic	X	X		X				X			X
Starward	X	X		X	X		X				
Stella Oceanis	X	X	X		X				X		
Stella Solaris	X	X	X		X						
Sun Viking	X	X		X							
Sunward II	X	X	X		X						
Tropicale	X	X		X	X		X	X	X	X	
Universe	X	X		X					X	X	X
Victoria	X	X	X		X					X	
Vistafjord	X	X		X	X	X	X	X	X	X	X
Westerdam	X	X	X		X	X	X	X	X	X	X
World Discoverer	X	X	X		X				X	X	X
Yorktown Clipper	X	X								X	
Crystal's Ship not named at Press Time	X	X		X	X	X	X	X	X	X	X

(*Not necessarily all cabins)

Note: Contact the appropriate cruise line for specific details regarding the information listed above.

Cruise Guide For Honeymooners

	Sunday/Monday Departures	Complimentary Champagne/Wine Reception	Complimentary Cake	Flowers	Table for Two	Double Bed or equivalent	Special Amenities
Admiral Cruises	•	•	•		•	•	Ship Ceremony & Photo
Aloha Pacific Cruises			•	•		•	
American Hawaii Cruises		•	•		•	•	Card from Captain & Certificate
Bermuda Star Line			•		•	•	Dinner at Captain's Table
Carnival Cruise Lines	•	•	•		•	•	Honeymoon Photo
Chandris Fantasy Cruises	•	•	•	•	•	•	Photo Album & Fruit Basket
Clipper Cruise Line		•	•		•		
Commodore Cruise Line		•				•	
Costa Cruises		•	•		•	•	
Crown Cruise Line	•	•	•		•	•	Dinner at Captain's Table–Photo
Crystal Cruises							
Cunard Line	•	•	•		•	•	Cocktail Party
Cunard/NAC	•	•	•		•	•	Cocktail Party
Cunard Sea Goddess	•	•	•	•	•	•	Comp. Cabin Bar, Fruit Basket
Delta Queen Steamboat Co.	•			•	•	•	
Dolphin Cruise Line	•	•	•		•	•	Captain's Cocktail Party; Commemorative Gift, Portrait, Photograph
Dolphin Hellas Cruises							
Epirotiki Lines		•	•	•	•	•	
Holland America Line	•	•	•	•	•	•	Silver Knife, Cocktail Party
Norwegian Cruise Line	•	•	•			•	Certificate, Photo & Cocktail Pty.
Ocean Cruise Lines	•	•	•		•	•	Cocktail Pty. & Fruit Basket
Pearl Cruises of Scandinavia	•		•		•	•	
Premier Cruise Lines	•	•	•		•	•	Certificate, Cocktail Party, Mock Ceremony, Photo Album, Crystal Wine Glasses
Princess Cruises/(Sitmar Cruises)	•		•		•		
Regency Cruises	•	•			•	•	Honeymoon Photo, Certificate, Surprise Gift
Royal Caribbean Cruise Line	•	•	•		•	•	Complimentary Cake
Royal Cruise Line	•	•	•		•	•	Complimentary Wine
Royal Viking Line		•	•	•		•	
Seabourn Cruise Line		•	•	•	•	•	
Sea Venture Cruises		•	•	•	•	•	Honeymoon Photo
Society Expeditions Cruises	•	•	•	•	•	•	Ship Ceremony, Certificate & Photo
Sun Line Cruises	•	•	•	•	•	•	
Windstar Sail Cruises	•	•	•		•	•	
World Explorer Cruises	•	•	•	•	•	•	Card from Captain & Photo

*Available in selected categories only.

Note: Request for amenities listed above must be indicated in advance of sailing, preferably at time of booking.

Cruise Guide For Children

	Admiral Cruises	Alaska Pacific Cruises	American Hawaii Cruises	Bermuda Star Line	Carnival Cruise Lines	Chandris Fantasy Cruises	Clipper Cruise Line	Commodore Cruise Line	Costa Cruise Line	Crown Cruise Line	Crystal Cruises	Cunard Line	Cunard Sea Goddess	Delta Queen Steamboat Co.	Dolphin Cruise Line	Epirotiki Lines	Holland America Line	Norwegian Cruise Line	Ocean Cruise Line	Pearl Cruises of Scandinavia	Premier Cruise Lines	Princess Cruises (Sitmar Cruises)	Regency Cruises	Royal Caribbean Cruise Line	Royal Viking Line	Seabourn Cruise Line	Sea Venture Line	Scandinavian Expedition Cruises	Sun Line Cruises	Windstar Sail Cruises	World Explorer Cruises
REDUCED CRUISE RATE (with 2 full-fare adults)(1)	A	A	A	A	A	A	A	A	A	A		A		A	A	A	A	A	A		A	A	A	A	A		A	A	A		A
AIR/SEA-RATE same or less as for full fare passengers	A	A	A	A	A	A		A	A			A			A	A	A	A	A		A	A	A	A			A	S			A
BABY SITTING AVAILABLE (2)	A	A	A		A	S		S	S			A		A	S		A	A	A		A	A	A		A		A		A		A
CRIBS AVAILABLE (3)	A	A	A		A	A		A	A			A		A	A		A	A	A		A	A	A	A	A		A	A	A		A
QUAD CABINS AVAILABLE	A	A	A	A	A	A		A	A			A		S	A	A	A	A	A		S	A	A	A	A		A	A	A		T
SPECIAL ACTIVITIES & SERVICES																															
Art & Craft Classes	A/H		A		A/H		A	A	S/H			A/H		A/H	S		S	A	A/H		S	A/H		A/H			S/H				A
Basketball	S				S		S	S				S			S		S	H	A		S	A		A							
Beach Parties	A	A/H	S		A/H			A/H	S/H			A/H		A/H	A/H		S	H	A		S	A/H		A			S/H				A
Bridge Tours						A																						A			A
Cartoons	A/H	A			A/H		A	H	S/H			A		A	A/H		S	A	A		S	A/H		A/H	A		S/H		A		A
Daily Paper	S			A				H	S			S		A	S		S/H	A	A		S	A			A		S/H	A	A		A
Dancing Classes			A/H		A		A	H	S					S			A/H	A	A		A/H	A					S/H				
Escorted Shore Tours			A		A		A	S	S								A/H	A	A		A/H	A									
Foreign Language Classes								S									A	H			A/H	S/H					A				A
Games & Contests	S		A		A		A	S	S/H			S/H			S/H		S	H	A		A/H	A/H		A/H	A/H						A
Hist. & Geo. Classes								S									A		A		A/H	S		A/H	A/H		S/H				A
Ice Cream Bar or Parties	A/H		A		A/H		A	S	S			S/H		S	S/H		S	H	A		A/H	A/H		A/H	A/H						A
Menus	A/H	A			A/H		A	A	S			A		S			A		A		A/H	A		A/H	H		S/H				A
Movies	A/H	A	A/H		A/H		A	A	A			A		S	A/H		S	H	A		A/H	A/H		A			S/H	A			A
Parties	S		A/H		A/H		A	A/H	H			A/H		S	A/H		S	H	A		A/H	A/H		A/H	S		S/H	A			A
Ping Pong	A		A		A		A	S	S			A			A/H		A	A	A		A	A		A			A/H				A
Pool (just for kids)	S		S		A		S	A	S			S			S		A		A		A/H	A		A			S/H				A
Snorkeling	S		S		A			A/H	S			A		A/H	A		A	A	A		A/H	A		A			S/H				A
Teen Center or Disco	S/H		A/H		A		A	A/H	A			S/H			A/H		H	A	A		A/H	A/H	S	A			S/H				
Teen Counselors	S/H		S/H		S		A	A	S			A			A/H		H	A	A		A/H	S/H	A/H				S/H				A
Video Games	A		A		A		A	S	H			A		A/H	A		A	A	A		A/H	A		A			S/H				
Volleyball							S	A	S			S			A		A	A	A		A	S		S			A				
Youth Center or Playroom	S		A		A		A	S	S			S		A	S		A	A	A		A	S		S	S					S	A
Youth Counselors	A/H	A/H	S/H		A/H		A/H	A	A/H			A/H		A	A/H		A	A	A		A/H	A/H	A	A/H			S/H				A/H

EXPLANATION KEY

A: All Ships
S: Some Ships and/or Destinations
T: No four-berth cabins available, but some triples.
H: Only seasonally; usually Christmas, Easter and Summer holiday periods. Whenever children are aboard, most ships go out of their way to accommodate them and their needs ... the more children on a sailing, the greater the variety of special activities.

(1) On most cruise lines, infants travel free. Where applicable, the maximum age for this rate ranges from 1 to 3 years.
(2) Where available, babysitting is arranged on-board.
(3) Where available, cribs arranged for at the time of booking.

The author, Capt. Bill Miller (left) with Richard Revnes, President of Royal Cruise Line, aboard the Crown Odyssey on her inaugural voyage of the Panama Canal

12

SAVE WITH GROUP SAILING RATES

Are you looking for that special cruise but having a hard time finding good rates? Perhaps your scheduled vacation time falls during the peak season. Or the cruise lines are not offering any discounts during your time off. Perhaps your work schedule does not allowed enough advance planning time for Advance Booking discounts.

Group Rates to the rescue.
You need to check out a travel agency that has group rates. Every good cruise travel agency worth it's salt should have group rates on several cruise sailings throughout the year. Group rates are usually 10% to 15% off the brochure rate and sometimes higher.

SHOPPING FOR GROUP RATE
Do group rates mean that you have to be a member of the organization that is going on the cruise?

No! Group rates are not always exclusively for organization members. Travel agents are usually happy to extend the group rates to people outside the club. Most advertising for an affinity group cruise will include a phrase like "special group rates are for members and their **"friends"**. "Friends" usually means anyone who has the bucks and wants to go.

Speculation Groups: Agents block space for a sailing date which they hope will sell well. Theme cruises and holidays are popular choices. The agent then advertises the cruise departure information in the newspaper and by direct mail.

ACTION:

Call all of your local travel agencies and be sure they have your name on their mailing list. If you live in a small town, be sure and get on the lists of agencies located in large cities near you. Watch for your local travel agency newspaper ads and check the big city Sunday papers.

"GG's" or Guaranteed Group Rates: Most travel agencies have a preferred cruise line that they enjoy selling. The agency and the cruise line develop an alliance. They call it a "preferred supplier relationship". The agency gets low group rates on several sailing dates . In return, the cruise line benefits with a steady flow of customers.

You benefit in several ways:

You are offered low group rates on a variety of dates and ships and destinations.

Your travel agent will become an expert on certain ships, instead of having to keep up with over 100 different vessels. This means you will have better information to base your decision on.

You will be the first to know abbout special discounts, last minute reduced rates etc. When a cruise line needs to fill up cabins on a slow selling cruise date, the first people they call are their preferred agencies. "Here are some rock bottom prices" they tell your agent, "Help us fill up some empty cabins on this slow date."

Don't you deserve to pay the lowest prices available?

ACTION:

Call local agencies and find out who their preferred suppliers are. Make a list of who each agency and who they use as their preferred suppliers. The next time you want to book a particular cruise line, you'll know which agency is likely to have the lowest rates or "GG's".

If you live in a small town, be sure that you get on the mailing lists of travel agencies located in large cities near you . You will find more information about locating discount travel agencies in the chapter about cruise magazines.

Sometimes Group Rate cruises will not be advertised in newspaper travel advertisements. Watch your newspaper for club news and social events for news of group cruise travel. Put your friends to work finding good cruise deals. Ask them to be on the lookout for any cruise specials. You'll have a hundred spies out bird dogging for those great rates.

13

ORGANIZE A GROUP AND SAIL FOR FREE

We know a lady who sails for FREE on cruise vacations several times a year. She never has to pay and she sails on all the best cruises.

How?

1 - She chooses a cruise ship & dateshe wants to sail on.
2 - She organizes friends and neighbors; who recognize the tremendous group rate savings, to join her on the cruise.
3 - Because she has organized the group, she sails for free on the Tour Conductor pass.
4 - This woman has successfully organized groups in the past.
5 - She has proven she can do the job so now she receive a small share of the commission.

She has become an outside sales agent

TOUR CONDUCTOR PASS
Most cruise lines give one free cruise fare for every 15 fares sold in group space. This free fare is referred to as a Tour Conductor Pass. The tour conductor fare provides free passage for the groups leader.

If you have a enough people your mate will also sail for free. This is how the cruise lines usually figure a group's tour conductor policy.

1 for 15 means the 16th person sails for free
I 2 for 30 means the 31st & 32nd passengers sail free
I 3 for 45 means the 46th, 47th, 48th passenger go freel

Port Tax is not included, everyone must pay this.

Note: 3rd and 4th passengers in a quad cabin are not usually counted towards a tour conductor pass.

Some cruise lines that currently have a policy of 1 free fare for every 15 passengers include:

American Hawaii Cruises
BSL Cruises
Carnival Cruise Line
Commodore Cruise Line
Costa Cruises
Dolphin Cruise Line
Holland America Line
Norwegian Cruise Line (NCL)
Princess Cruises
Royal Cruise Line

Getting Started

Working with a local Travel Agent

If your ambitious and ready to organize a group, you'll need to find a good travel agent. You need an agent who will teach you good skills. The agent must be someone who you will feel comfortable working with.

Visit the travel agencies in your area. Ask them how they work with group leaders and outside sales people. Selling travel may develop into a profitable part time job.

Travel agents welcome potential group leaders, but past experience has made them careful. Until you prove yourself, they will probably have a "show me what you can do" attitude.

New group leaders with limited experience are rewarded with tour a conductor pass.

The Cruise
You will choose a ship and date for your group to sail on. The agency will negotiate a group contract with the cruise line. The travel agent will help you to understand deposit deadlines and how to explain the brochure so you can effectively sell the cruise to your clients.

ACTION: Organizing a group can be as simple as calling all of your friends.

Call your friend "Marge."
"Hello Marge, you know how we had been talking about doing something special this year...Well you won't believe what a terrific cruise deal I've come across. It's on that fabulous ------ sailing from Miami and we'll save tons of money off the regular rate."

"You mean that cruise that's always on the TV advertisements?" says Marge.

"Yep that's the one, a 7-night cruise to the Caribbean with everything included" you say.

"Just imagine all the food!" say's Marge, "The midnight buffets, and the impeccable service! I won't have to cook!

"The guys can play golf on the islands, And with the 27% that will save off the cruise price we can do some great duty free shopping in St.Thomas." you remind her.

"WOW! Sounds terrific" says Marge.

"It really is a fabulous deal, but to get these great rates we'll have to get at least 7 couples to go." you tell her. " "Besides, it's more fun to cruise with a bunch of friends. Remember when we all went on that day trip together?''

"Yeah, we'll have to let everybody know" says Marge. "This is gonna be great."

You have just planted the seed. Next, tell everyone you know about the terrific deal on the cruise. **Invite them to join you.** Tell your butcher, hairdresser, minister, the insurance man, dry cleaners, the people at the library. Tell the society column writer at the local paper. TELL EVERYONE!

See-EM'....Tell-EM'....Sell-EM'

Here are 12 good prospects for group cruise sales.

1 - Alumni Associations
2 - Service Clubs (Lions, Rotary)
3 - Condo and Mobile Home Groups
4 - Employee Clubs
5 - Friends & Family
6 - Family Reunions
7 - Occupational Trade Groups
8 - Professional Groups (doctors, nurses,lawers,teachers)
9 - Religious Groups
10 - Schools
11 - Sororities & Fraternities
12 - Special Interest Groups (bridge club, garden, computer)

WORKING AS AN OUTSIDE SALES AGENT

With experience, you will become more valuable to the travel agency. You will begin to receive more benefits and share in commissions. Productive outside sales agents go on free or nearly free Familiarization Trips. (Fam trips)

Compensation should be discussed with the agency owner before you start working.

Remember to take your time choosing the agency you'll want to work with. Your new part time job should be fun. It is important that the people you work with are fair and have a sense of humor.

By acting as a commissioned outside sales agent you become your own small business. A small business makes a great **TAX SHELTER**.

Operating a small business will allow you to deduct expenses when filing taxes with the Internal Revenue Service. Deductible expenses may include the following:

    *automobile expenses
    *business equipment (vcr's, computers)
    *answering service
    *magazine subscriptions
    *telephone bills
    *printing bills (fliers, stationary)
    *health club & country club memberships.

ACTION TIP:
Get the book ''Wealth Without Risk'' by Charles Givens. Givens has some excellent ideas on how to build a fortune without going out on a limb. Chapter 13 in the book is called ''Travel the World on Deductible Dollars''. Givens says that you should start a small business for fun, profit and huge tax deductions. I agree!

You can receive a Free information package by calling the Charles J. Givens Organization at 800-548-8525 or write to them at 921 Douglas Ave. , Altmont Springs, Fl. 32714.

14

"I'M MAD AS HELL
AND I'M NOT GONNA TAKE IT ANYMORE!"

Attention Single Travellers! If you've felt like this after paying extra to travel single occupancy, you're not alone.

Single passengers have been discriminated against for years. Cruise lines, hotels and resorts are all guilty of adding on expensive surcharges onto singles passengers fares.

As a single traveller, you've had no choice. You paid extra or you missed the boat.

Cruise lines complain that they lose revenue by selling a cabin to one passenger instead of two. To make up for this loss, they charge the innocent single passenger 150% to 200% of the regular cruise rate.

150% is the cruise fare + 1/2 of a fare.
200% is double, or like paying for an invisible 2nd passenger.

Ouch! This can really hurt a persons vacation budget.

Good News For The Single Traveler

Cabin Share & Roommate Programs

Today, most cruise lines offer cabin share or roommate programs to accommodate the single traveler.

If you feel uncomfortable with the thought of sharing a cabin with someone. Your not alone. Many people have felt the same way before they sailed in a roommate program. However, they found after they gave the roommate program a try, that they genuinely enjoyed it.

If you're single, you owe it to yourself to try a roommate share program. You will discover that you have a lot in common with the other singles in the roommate program. Most of the singles you meet on cruises have interests and goals similar to your own. And like you, they are looking for a cruise at a reasonable price.

Roommate programs are reminiscent of a college dorm. You're only in the cabin to change clothes, shower and sleep. Cruise ships are big enough so that you won't be ''stuck'' with your roommate once you leave the cabin.

The first night of the cruise will usually include a singles ''meet and greet'' Happy Hour. You'll have a chance to spot the other passengers who are unattached. Throughout the cruise, activities and entertainment events are designed to enhance your cruise experience.

By the time the cruise is over you will have made many new friends and maybe a new love interest.

HOT ACTION TIP:
Landry & Kling, world famous cruise specialists from Coral Gables, Florida suggest ''On most ships the photographer will take pictures of all passengers as they first come aboard the ship. If you look over these photos when they are displayed in the photo gallery, you can see who's traveling with whom, and who's traveling alone.''

Landry & Kling, Inc. has a informative booklet of cruise hints; "100 Hints to Enhance Your Cruise." Send $2.00 to Landry & Kling, Inc.; Hints Dept. "B", 1390 South Dixie Highway, Suite 1207, Coral Gables, Fl. 33146. Landry & Kling also have a toll free number for reservations 800-431-4007.

Note: Single Women Travelers

Cruises are a safe way for single women to travel. You can relax in the public rooms of the ship and feel comfortable. The ambience of cruise ships allows you to make new friends easily without pressure. Some cruise lines offer special Host programs for single woman travelers, (see ROYAL CRUISE LINE HOST PROGRAM, chapter 15.

Booking the Cabin

When you book, you may be given the choice of an inside or an outside cabin. If you choose an outside cabin with a porthole you usually have to pay a little extra.

Most of the cabins cruise lines use for roommate programs are called "run of ship" cabins. "Run of ship" simply means that the cruise line will put you where they want to.

Hey, who cares? All the cabins are going to the same ports! Take the money you'll save and spend it in the gift shop buying a present for that new "significant other" you've just met.

ACTION TIP:

2nd Seating for Dinner is the favorite choice for singles. This gives you more time to relax in the different lounges and public rooms before dinner. Have your travel agent request a large table when making your dining arrangements. Request that you be placed at a table of singles if possible.

SINGLES GUARANTEED SHARE PROGRAMS

Guaranteed share programs are offered by several of the major cruise lines. The cruise line will match you up with other single passengers of the same sex and if possible, in the same age group. Cruise lines use double occupancy and quad(4) occupancy cabins.

Single Occupancy Cabins

A few of the cruise lines are now offering single occupancy cabins for only a small amount above the regular rate. American Hawaii Cruises, Premier Cruises and Royal Caribbean Cruise Line have some of the best deals for the passenger who wants a private cabin.

SINGLES PROGRAMS FROM 1989 BROCHURES
(port charges not included and are extra).

ADMIRAL CRUISES: Fare + 50% - No share program

AMAZON RIVER CRUISES: "Cabin Share Program" Double occupancy cabins are available at brochure rate. Single occupancy cabins, Fare + 81% (Amazon River cruises are not for wimps. This may be one of the most interesting cruises you will ever take.)

AMERICAN CRUISE LINE: "Cabin Share Program" Double occupancy cabins are available at brochure rate. Subject to availability. Single Occupancy cabins, Fare + 20%

AMERICAN HAWAII CRUISES: 7- Night Hawaiian Island Cruise. Single occupancy of cabins in category "C" and "G" are available at no extra charge. Category "C" outside cabin $1,995 cruise only rate. Category "G" inside cabin $1,650 cruise only rate.

BSL CRUISES (formerly BERMUDA STAR LINE): "Guaranteed Share Program" You may request a particular cabin category. Bermuda Star will try to match a roommate of same sex based on age & smoking preference. Upper/Lower berth cabins not available. You pay the brochure rate for the category in which you are assigned.
Single occupancy cabin rate, Fare + 50%

CARNIVAL CRUISE LINE: "Singles Plan" - 4 to cabin; 3 day cruise is $275; 4 day cruise is $395; 7 day cruise is $595. Carnival has a very good program for singles! These are cruise only rates, Air/sea connections are not available.
Single occupancy in cabin 200% - you pay double

CHANDRIS FANTASY CRUISES: "Single Saver" Quad share program - You pay a guaranteed quad share rate, this rate is less then the least expensive cruise fare.

COMMODORE CRUISE LINE: "Commodore Roommate" 2 to a cabin only; pay the rate listed for the category your booked.
Single occupancy in cabin, Fare + 50%.

CUNARD: "Guaranteed Share" available only on Cunard Countess and Cunard Princess. Pay the rate of cabin category you are assigned.
Single occupancy in cabin, Fare + 75%.

DELTA QUEEN STEAMBOAT CO.: "Guaranteed Share" Available only in Category "D" on both Delta Queen and Mississippi Queen steamboats. You pay Category "D" rate. Inside cabin with 2 lower beds. Single occupancy in cabin, Fare + 50%.

EPIROTIKI: "Guaranteed Share" Double occupancy cabins are available at brochure rate. Subject to availability.
Single Occupancy cabins, Fare + 50%.

EXPRINTER CRUISES: Single occupancy cabin, Fare + 50%
Unique & interesting way to see Europe by river.

FLOATING THROUGH EUROPE: Single occupancy cabins are available for about $200 above the double occupancy rate.
Small River barges with cozy atmosphere - and are able to navigate the narrower European waterways.

HOLLAND AMERICA LINE: "Guaranteed Share" a limited number of double occupancy cabins are available. Cruise line decides which cabin you get. You pay the rate of the category your cabin is located in. On the Nieuw Amsterdam and Noordam, cabins are available in category "E" through "J." On the Westerdam cabins are in category "F" through "L." On the Rotterdam, category "E" through "M."
On the Rotterdam single occupancy cabins are available in Cat. Q & R. On the Nieuw Amsterdam, Noordam & Westerdam, single occupancy cabins vary from 150% to 200%.

NORWEGIAN CRUISE LINE: "Guaranteed Quad-Share" 4 to a cabin age 18 and over; 7 day cruises $650 per person; 7 day SS Norway cruise $695; The air/sea program does not apply.
Single occupancy cabins - some "run of ship" cabins may be available depending on ship - Fare varies. Passengers requesting single occupancy in a specific category will be charged 150% - 200%.

PAQUET FRENCH CRUISE: Single occupancy cabin, Fare + 50% No share program.

PREMIER CRUISE LINE: Premier has an excellent program for the single passenger or the SINGLE PARENT. There are limited cabins set aside for the single passenger at no extra charge. (Cabins are usually priced at the lowest rate in the brochure. SINGLE PARENT - pays the same low rate as the single passenger and can take along up to 3 children. Each child travels at the 3/4 passenger rate. Good Deal!! Book early!
As the official cruise line for Walt Disney World, Premier has an excellent program for children. Premier defines a child as a passenger under the age of 18.

PRINCESS CRUISES: "Guaranteed Share Program" Very limited availability on sailing dates. Single passenger is restricted in choice of cabin categories. Call for current information and don't get your hopes up.
Single occupancy cabin, Fare + 25%.

REGENCY CRUISE LINE: "Regency Roommate Program" Share a double occupancy cabin at the brochure rate. Regency will choose the cabin. Regency is very good about upgrading passengers. There are some single occupancy cabins available that don't cost that much extra. The more expensive cabins: single occupancy rate is Fare + 30% to 50%.

ROYAL CRUISE LINE: Single occupancy cabins are limited and available only on some sailings. The cost is $50.00 extra per day.
Royal Cruise Line does a fabulous job of making the single woman passenger feel comfortable.(See Royal Cruise Line Host Program)

Royal Cruise Line does a fabulous job of making the single woman passenger feel comfortable.(See Royal Cruise Line Host Program)

ROYAL CARIBBEAN CRUISE LINE:
The readers of Travel-Holiday magazine have voted RCCL "the world's best cruise line" five years in a row!

"Guaranteed Single Occupancy Fare"
Single occupancy of a stateroom. Excellent program! You pay only a small 15% percent above the lowest priced cabin on the ship **if you sail during the off season.** If you sail during the peak season you pay 33% above the lowest priced cabin. You will be assigned a "run of ship" cabin at embarkation. You can expect to get a very nice cabin, there are not any inferior cabins on RCCL ships.

"Special Share Program" Passengers who would like to share a cabin may do so at the rate of an "A" deck inside cabin, less $5.00. "A" deck cabins are inexpensive and an excellent value! Your stateroom will be assigned at embarkation, and at the discretion of the company.

ROYAL VIKING: On Royal Viking Sea, Royal Viking Sky & Royal Viking Star single occupancy in specific cabins is Fare + 40%
On Royal Viking Sun single occupancy in Category "B1" through "J1" is Fare + 60% . Space is limited and subject to availability.

SUN LINE: "Cabin Share Program" Double occupancy cabins are occasionally available at the brochure rate. The New York office has to telex Greece to check arrangements. Inquire in advance. Single occupancy cabins, Fare + 50% or more.

VENICE SIMPLON ORIENT EXPRESS: There are substantial savings in single occupancy fares if you sail during the Off Season, mid September to late October. The 1989 rate was $1,392 for an inside cabin in category C. call 800-524-2420.

15

SINGLEWORLD

Recently aboard Royal Caribbean Cruise Lines "Sovereign Of The Seas" there was one group that seemed to be having a particularly good time. You'd see them by the pool on the top deck of the ship having champagne parties. Or late at night they would all be at the midnight buffet telling stories and laughing. They were part of a Singleworld cruise group.

Wendy Lowenstein of Singleworld describes it best; "When you go on big ships like the SS Norway, the Sovereign of the Seas or Carnival's Superliners, you are one person among 1,200. Traveling with Singleworld, you'll instantly make 35 or 40 new friends. We start things off with a welcome aboard cocktail party and throughout the cruise we schedule events designed to make your vacation special."

THE SINGLEWORLD ADVANTAGE
Singleworld cruiser has several unique advantages.
"Our escorts sail on the ships regularly. They work closely with the cruise ships staff. If you need anything, your Singleworld escort can arrange it quickly."

Lowenstein says Singleworld escorts are experts on the ports of call. "With over 500 departures a year, Singleworld groups are in different ports every week. Our escorts know the good stores to shop.

Our shore excursions are more fun and party oriented then the regular ones offered by the ships. We might go sailing in St. Maarten or throw a beach party in Barbados.''

SingleWorld also offers single share trips to Hawaii and Europe.

THE SINGLEWORLD CLUB

Singleworld is a membership club. Anyone who is single or traveling alone is eligible for membership. The annual dues are $20.00. You are not required to pay dues until you actually book a cruise. SingleWorld will match you with a cabin mate of your own sex and age group. This is similar to guaranteed cabin share programs offered by the cruise lines.

This is the 32nd year SingleWorld has been in business Singleworld promotes over 10 group cruise departures a week. Over 234,000 people of **all age groups** have cruised with Singleworld.

Singleworld's main market is the single traveller between the ages of 20 to 35. There are special departures for members in this age group. They also have ''All Ages'' departures for all single people. SingleWorld is becoming more popular with mature travellers. I have booked many senior citizens who are happy repeat SingleWorld passengers.

If you are single and don't care for group activities, that's OK too. You don't have to take part in any of SingleWorld's activity on the cruise if you don't want to.

Because SingleWorld does such a volume business with the cruise lines, they get excellent rates for their club members. Low cruise fares include air transportation. (Cruise Only rates are available)

Check into the good deals that this company is offering the single traveller. Call toll free to get your **FREE** copy of SingleWorld's colorful cruise brochure. 800-223-6490 Or write to SingleWorld, 401 Theodore Fremd Avenue, Rye, New York 10580.

SingleWorld requests you make your cruises reservations through your local travel agent. There is no extra charge for using travel agents.

16

ROYAL CRUISE LINE HOST PROGRAM

* Gallant Gentlemen Sail For FREE! *

Imagine seeing an ad in a cruise magazine like this:

"Wanted: Charming, distinguished gentleman to provide gallant partnership to unescorted lady guests. Dancing, dining, shore excursions, parties, card games and musical shows aboard a free luxury cruise ship and absolutely free."

If it sounds like a great way for a semi-retired gentleman to spend a few weeks, you're right. Royal Cruise Line's "Host Program" is into it's sixth successful year. The program was pioneered by Richard Revnes, president of Royal Cruise Line.

"My wife Christa used to point out the disproportion of single, mature women to single men aboard ships." says Revnes. " When we traveled on many cruises my wife would have me dance with all the single, older woman and it just plain wore me out"
"But we also saw how many of the never had a chance to dance. Dancing is a very enjoyable and important part of the cruise for women."

Royal Cruise Line Host Program

More than 200 gentlemen, extensively interviewed by Royal Cruise, make up the host program. These charming men, mostly retired from the fields of medicine, law, business and the military join the Golden Odyssey & Crown Odyssey as invited friends. They are not paid, professional hosts.

A ratio of one host to ten single ladies aboard is the general rule. The hosts give the lady passengers who sail alone, someone with whom she can share the excitement of the cruise

I have sailed aboard the Crown Odyssey and have seen the host program in action and it's terrific. The women enjoy being pampered with attention. No woman sits in a lounge very long before an attractive host in a dinner jacket asks her for a dance. These fellows work hard but it's obvious they are also enjoying themselves.

Hosts can expect to sail 3-4 weeks a year and sometimes longer. You are given a booklet of do's and don'ts. The cruise line encourages you to dress fashionably. At dinner you will be seated at large tables consisting of single woman.

You are expected to keep circulating because of the ratio of one host for every 10 single women. Dancing with different women is a must. When you are in port you will go on the shore excursions. While at sea you'll be busy attending lectures, bingo and playing cards.

I've seen the hosts helping out the crew and cruise director with all types of activities. A couple of the guys helped run the spotlights during one of the nightly shows. Being a host is like being part of the cast in a show. Everyone pitch's in to make it a smash hit.

The hosts enjoy a wonderful time and they sail for free.

ACTION: Royal Cruise Line accepts no applications directly. Men must be recommended by travel agents. This is because Royal Cruise takes the view that the travel agent has a vested interest in supplying only the best hosts. Your travel agency will handle the preliminary screening, a personal interview is then arranged by the cruise line.

17

ELEVEN REASONS TO CONVINCE MARRIED MEN TO TAKE THEIR "FIRST" CRUISE
By Richard Revnes
President, Royal Cruise Line

1. **HE WILL NOT BE BORED**
   Cruising is a great Sea Adventure with new ports of call to explore each day.

2. **HE CAN PLAY GOLF OR TENNIS**
   Urge him to take his clubs or racquet. Most Caribbean, Mexican and even Mediterranean ports ofcall have facilities and arrangements to play can be made.

3. **HE DOES NOT HAVE TO DRESS UP**
   (unless he chooses to) Cruising today is very informal, he can dress insports wear without a tie most of the time.

4. **NO DECISIONS TO MAKE**
   No airline schedules to reconfirm every few days -- no restaurants to select, no schedules to plan.

5. **CAN GO TO BED WHEN HE WANTS**
   If wife wants to stay up, he cango to bed or vice-versa, no problem.

6. **NO NEW LANGUAGE OR FOREIGN CURRENCY TO LEARN**
   On board ship, American currency or credit cards are always used and also accepted in most ports of call.

7. NO CONTINUOUS TIPPING
On most ships, tipping is done once at the end of the cruise.

8. EATS WHAT HE WANTS!
No decisions to make -- he can have steak every day if he wants. No exotic dishes to explore unless he wants to.

9. NO REGIMENTATION
He is boss; he does what he wantswith his time. He doesn't have to take shore excursions or participate in anything unless he wants to.

10. INDEPENDENT ACTIVITIES
He can participate in things he likes to do (golf lessons, reading, bingo, movies, etc.)while his wife does her thing - bridge, bingo, dance lessons, etc.

11. HE WILL NOT GET SEASICK
Many men who were in World War II aboard Navy ships or transports were deathly sick. Those ships **did not** have stabilizers as all modern cruise ships have. Today, there are many new drugs on the market which prevent seasickness.

18

CRUISE MAGAZINES &
FINDING DISCOUNT TRAVEL AGENCIES

Subscribe to magazine dedicated to cruises.

The better informed you are about the different cruise lines, the more intelligently you will be able to plan your dream vacation. Read the latest cruise magazines and you'll be able to spot all the money-saving cruise deals.

Two popular magazines are exclusively devoted to cruising; **Cruise Magazine** and **Cruise Travel**. Both offer informative stories on the cruise industry. Each issue, the magazines focus on different ships cruising the seven seas. New ships are profiled and older ships are revisited.

You need to start reading **Cruise Magazine** today. They bill themselves as ''The Cruise Enthusiasts Magazine.'' Gary Workman, editor of Cruise Magazine says, ''We like to give the reader an interesting, in-depth look at cruise ships. We're not into ''hype and fluff'' stories. We love the cruise industry. We want our readers to have the best information so they can make the right choices.''

Cruise Magazine is published bimonthly. Look for the destination guide published in each issue. The destination guide is in the form of a chart. Ships are profiled according to their destination. For example, all ships cruising to Alaska would be listed together.

A quick glance will tell you the port of departure, average brochure fare and ship specifications such as size, ship's age, crew nationality etc. The destination guide also lists sailing dates and itinerary.

Each issue of Cruise Magazine has a special section that lists travel agents around the country that specialize in cruises. Many of the agencies listed have toll free numbers. Call or write these travel agencies and get on their mailing lists.

Cruise Magazine is well worth your money. If your newsstand dealer does not have it, ask him to order it. Or you can Save 25% OFF the cover price with an inexpensive subscription.
Call Cruise Magazines subscription Hotline 1-800-888-6088.

Cruise Travel Magazine: is another valuable resource. This bi-monthly magazine is produced by World Publishing Company in Illinois. World Publishing also publishes **Tours and Resorts.**

Cruise Travel has been in business for over 10 years. Each issue features a Port of the Month, Ship of the Month and Cruise of the Month profile.

Subscriptions are available by writing: Cruise Travel Magazine, P.O. Box 3767, Escondido, Ca. 92025-9690. Or complete a business reply card from an issue of **Cruise Travel Magazine.**

Watch Cruise Magazines for
Discount Travel Agency Advertisements

Interested in saving money? Check your cruise magazine for Discount Travel Agency advertisements. Discount agencies advertise incredible discounts - up to 50% savings! They rarely list actual sailing dates; so interested travelers must call for details. This is a good chance for you to get on their mailing list.

The Role of Discount Travel Agencies.

The cruise lines often rely on discount agencies to help sell last minute empty cabin space. These agencies do volume business and they frequently get snake-belly-low rates. The discount agencies are also able to offer low rates because of "preferred supplier relationship" with a cruise line.

Each agency works with several preferred suppliers. If Carnival is their preferred supplier, they will brag they have the best deals on Carnival. Once you have a good idea which cruise line you'd like to sail with, check the ad's to see who is selling your cruise line.

ACTION:
* Telephone the discount agencies and ask to have your name added to their mailing list

* Ask if the agency is bonded. Are they a member of a major travel agent association like CLIA, NACOA, or ASTA?

* Ask if there is there a membership charge or extra fees.

Important Questions to Ask Before you Book:
* Does the agency accept credit cards? Which cards are accepted?

* What is the Cruise Cancellation Policy. (Be sure they explain it so you can understand it.)

* If you purchase Cancellation Insurance or Health Insurance, be sure you understand these policies also.

* When will you receive your tickets?

Why Use a Credit Card?
With all the scare stories about credit card fraud most people have become cautious about giving their credit card number over the phone. If you are certain that you are dealing with a legitimate agency, go ahead and use your credit card to make the cruise fare purchase.

Credit cards make it easier for you to obtain refunds. Credit cards also offer you the best protection when you are dealing with an out-of-state company.

If you pay by check you could have problems. If you needed to get a refund or dispute a charge, try dealing with a company located half-way across the country after they have already cashed your che

Federal regulations make credit the preferred method of payment. The Federal Fair Credit Billing Act states that consumers are not liable for goods and services not delivered as agreed. If a problem occurs, you have 60 days after receiving your bill to write the credit card company and dispute the charge.

In 1988, Exploration Cruise Line filed for bankruptcy. The people who had bought their ticket with a credit card were protected. So were the ones who had the trip cancellation insurance. The other poor souls who paid by check are having a difficult time trying to get their money back.

A Final Word

Shop locally for the cruise deal you want before you spend your money out of town.

Many local agents also have a preferred supplier relationship with cruise lines, just like the big discount agencies. Check out your local agencies first. If you are working with your local agent and trouble develops, you can always go to the office and stamp your feet. Try doing that over a long distance phone line.

Before you book with an out of state agency, **check with your local agents first.**

FREE OFFER FROM AMERICAN EXPRESS

The American Express company has been a leader in the travel industry for decades. They are famous for the American Express credit card slogan "Don't leave home without it."

American Express is now offering a beautiful full color brochure called "The American Express Cruise Decision Kit" This brochure has 24 pages of neat cruise tips. Don't leave home without a free copy of "The American Express Cruise Decision Kit."

A limited number of the cruise decision kits are still available from American Express. Write to:"American Express Cruise Decision Kit" P.O. Box 9035, East Setauket, N.Y. 11733-9035. Be sure to indicate if you are an American Express Individual card member or Gold card member.

19

BUYING BARTERED TRAVEL BARGAINS

You can save up to 50% off your next vacation by purchasing bartered travel.

What is bartered travel?

Instead of paying cash for advertising, airlines, cruise lines, hotels, car rental companies and restaurants frequently pay for advertising with barter. They issue credit for future services - airline tickets, cruise tickets, hotel rooms etc.

The advertising agency resells the travel vendors credits to you at a steeply discounted rate.

MAKING A RESERVATION

When you call a barter company you should be ready to supply some basic information on your travel plans. This information will help the reservation agent to better serve you.

Airline: departure airport, airline, flight number, departure time, destination and number of people. Call the airlines in advance to get this information.

Cruise ship: name of cruise line & ship, sailing date, type of cabin. (inside or outside cabin)

Call the barter agency with this information. If they have credit with that travel supplier, they will give you a discounted price and make the reservations. The tickets will be in your name. You will be treated like a regular passenger when you check-in.

If you have not already chosen a destination...
Give the barter companies a call. See what they have to offer. You can't get lucky if you don't try. They may be holding barter on a terrific destination that you might never have thought of.

WARNING

Cancellation: Be sure that you understand the cancellation penalties when you purchase anything through a barter company.

Most barter companies will assume the same cancellation conditions and penalties of the vendor.(cruise line, airlines etc.) Most vendors have strict cancellation policies with expensive penalties. Check the vendors brochure for cancellation policies before you book.

Buying Small Ticket Items
You can also save money when you purchase small ticket items. With restaurant meals or hotel rooms, you will probably use a form of payment called "script". Script is like paper money and it is redeemable for it's face value.

For Example:
You visit a restaurant and order your dinner in the usual fashion. At the end of the meal your check is presented. You give the waiter your script certificates. If your check amounts to $61.00, you would give the waiter six $10.00 script certificates and one dollar in cash.

You never receive change back when you use script. All taxes and tips must be paid for in cash.

Three Barter Companies Ready To Save You Money

ALL Advertising Associates, Inc / Lino and Associates,
5665 Central Ave.; St.Petersburg, Fl. 33710 (phone 813--384-6700)
All Advertising barters with airlines, car rental companies, cruise ship lines, motel/hotel chains, land tour operators, resorts and restaurants in cities across the United States.

"Our inventory of available travel specials is constantly changing" says Fred Lino, Jr. President of ALL Advertising, "Give us a call and see what's available."

The people at ALL are nice folks to do business with. Call or write ALL and ask to be put on their mailing list. No membership fee.

Communications Development Corp (CDC) 1454 Euclid St., Santa Monica, California,(phone 213-458-0596) Barters with airlines, car rental companies, cruise ship lines, motel/hotel chains, land tour operators, resorts and restaurants in cities across the United States. Write to CDC and ask to be put on their mailing list. No membership fee.

"Reciprocal Merchandising Services" 225 W. 34th St. Suite 2203, New York, N.Y. 10122. 212-244-3562 Dues $50.00 per year.
Airfares: 25-40% discount. Club provides across-the-board discounts on any ticket, Maxsaver to First Class from major US airlines. 25% discount on Europe based transatlantic charter airlines.
Cruises: 25% or more discount. Club brochure lists 18 major cruise lines.

Hotels: 25-50% discount. Club brochure lists 5 major chains plus about 100 hotels in CA, CT, FL, HI, NJ NY, PA and other states. Bermuda, Mexico and the Caribbean.

Restaurants: 30% discount on dinners and beverages at over 250 restaurants in New York City. Other major cities including: Chicago, Los Angles, Miami, Philadelphia, San Francisco.

Other: Package tours, Health clubs, car rentals, furniture, and miscellaneous retail merchandise.

ACTION TIP: Barter companies offer you a no frills opportunity to buy discount travel. Barter companies do not have time to worry about getting you a refund for cancelled travel.

* BE CERTAIN THAT YOU CAN MAKE THE TRIP
BEFORE   YOU BOOK!

* CONSIDER TRIP CANCELLATION INSURANCE

INSURANCE

There are many good companies offering cancellation insurance and t   For a Free brochure that will   :ading, Penns   explain the types and costs of   . The broch   travel insurance please call   oes are availa   toll-free 1-800-826-1300   Thanks, :m you read a   Capt. Bill Miller 4-2-90   NTS".

20

Money Saving Checklist

OFF SEASON

* When possible, always cruise during the Off Season.

* Use Early Booking Discounts

* Consider sailing on a repositioning cruise - Look for special past passenger disounts and early booking discounts on repositioning cruises.

* Watch the Travel section of major newspapers for special discounts on slow selling cruise dates. (Get a Florida newspaper if possible)

* Book a SeaSavers Cruise

* Try American Hawaii Standby Program

* Write to all cruise lines and get on their mailing list.

* Join cruise line passenger clubs and be sure that your on their mailing list.

* Use discounts and upgrades available to past passengers.

* Get on local and national travel agency mailing lists. (you need to hear about all the available group rates and specials)

* Have your travel agent check with cruise lines for week of sailing reduced rates. (you must be less then a week away from sailing date)

IF YOU MUST SAIL DURING ON SEASON

* Check with travel agents for group departure rates.

* Have your travel agent check with cruise lines for week of sailing reduced rates. (you must be less then a week away from sailing date)

* When your travel agent calls a cruise line to check on information, be sure that they mention that you are a past passenger. You don't want to miss any specials that are available only to past passengers.

* Check for SeaSavers

* Check with barter firms for discounted rates.

* Consider a Pier Head Jump.

BIBLIOGRAPHY

John Maxtone Graham
(Excellent Nautical Author)
-Liners to the Sun
-S.S. Norway
-The Only Way to Cross
-Dark Brown is the River
-Olympic & Titanic

The Path Between The Seas
David McCullough, Simon & Schuster

The Total Traveler By Ship
Ethel Blum (Excellent Book)
P.O Box 41-4298,
Miami Bch. Fl.33141-0298

Berlitz Complete Handbook to Cruising
Douglas Ward
MacMillan Publishing

The Cruise Answer Book
Charlanne Fields Herring
Mills & Sanderson Publishing

Fieldings Worldwide Cruises
Antoinette Deland
Wm. Morrow & Co.

Frommer's Dollarwise Cruises
Marlyn Springer & Donald Schultz
Prentice Hall

New World Of Travel (Excellent)
Arthur Frommer
Prentice Hall

Nothing Can Go Wrong
John D. MacDonald & Capt. John Kilpack
Fawcett Crest

2 EXCELLENT PASSENGER ORGANIZATIONS
You should consider joining

World Ocean and Cruise Liner Society
"Ocean and Cruise News" monthly newsletter
P.O. Box 92
Stamford, Ct. 06480

International Cruise Passenger Association
"Cruise Digest" bimonthly newsletter
P.O. Box 886 FDR Station
New York, N.Y. 10150-0886

CRUISE LINE EXECUTIVE OFFICES

NOTES

ADMIRAL CRUISES
1220 Biscayne Blvd.
Miami, Fl. 33132

AMERICAN CRUISE LINE
1 Marine Park
Haddam, Ct. 06438

AMERICAN HAWAII CRUISES
550 Kearny St. #501
San Francisco, Ca. 94108

AMAZON RIVER CRUISES
1013 S. Central Ave
Glendale, Ca. 91204

BSL CRUISES (Bermuda Star)
1086 Teaneck Rd.
Teaneck, N.J. 07666

CANBERRA CRUISES
77 New Oxford St.
London, England WC1A-1PP

CARNIVAL CRUISE LINE
5225 N.W. 87th Ave.
Miami, Fl. 33178

CHANDRIS FANTASY CRUISES
900 Third Ave.
New York, N.Y. 10022

CLIPPER CRUISE LINE
7711 Bonhomme Ave.
St. Louis, Mo. 63105

COMMODORE CRUISE LINE
1007 North America Way
Miami, Fl. 33132

COSTA CRUISES
80 S.W. 8th St.
Miami, Fl. 33130

CROWN CRUISE LINE
2790 N. Federal Highway
Boca Raton, Fl. 33431

CRYSTAL CRUISES
2121 Ave. of the Stars #200
Los Angles, Ca. 90067

CUNARD LINE
555 Fifth Avenue
New York, N.Y. 10017

DELTA QUEEN STEAMBOAT CO.
30 Robin St. Wharf
New Orleans, La. 70130

DOLPHIN CRUISE LINE
1007 North America Way
Miami, Fl. 33132

EPIROTIKI LINE
551 Fifth Ave. #605
New York, N.Y. 10176

EXPRINTER CRUISES
500 Fifth Ave.
New York, N.Y. 10110

FLOATING THROUGH EUROPE
271 Madison Ave #1007
New York, N.Y. 10024

NOTES

GALAPAGOS CENTER
156 Giralda Ave.
Coral Gables, Fl. 33134

**HILTON INTERNATIONAL/
NILE CRUISES**
605 Third Ave.
New York, N.Y. 10158

HOLLAND AMERICA LINE/WESTOURS
300 Elliot Ave W.
Seattle, Wa. 98119

HORIZON CRUISES
16000 Ventura Blvd.
Encino, Ca. 91436

NORWEGIAN CRUISE LINE (NCL)
95 Merrick Way
Coral Gables, Fl. 33134

OCEAN & PEARL CRUISE LINES
1510 S.E. 17th St.
Fort Lauderdale, Fl. 33316

PREMIER CRUISE LINE
P.O. Box 573
Cape Canaveral, Fl. 32920

PRINCESS CRUISES
2029 Century Park East
Los Angles, Ca. 90067

REGENCY CRUISE
260 Madison Ave.
New York, N.Y. 10016

Royal Caribbean Cruise Line
903 South America Way
Miami, Fl. 33132

ROYAL CRUISE LINE
1 Maritime Plaza
San Francisco, Ca. 94111

ROYAL VIKING LINE
95 Merrick Way
Coral Gables, Fl. 33134

SEABOURNE CRUISE LINE
55 Francisco St. #710
San Francisco, Ca. 94133

SOCIETY EXPEDITIONS
3131 Elliot Ave. #700
Seattle, Wa. 98121

SUN LINE CRUISES
1 Rockefeller Plaza #315
New York, N.Y. 10020

VENICE SIMPLON ORIENT EXPRESS
One World Trade Center #2565
New York, N.Y. 10048

WINDSTAR CRUISES
300 Elliot Ave. West
Seattle, Wa. 98119

WORLD EXPLORER CRUISES
555 Montgomery St.
San Francisco, Ca. 94111

Glossary

Above Board - Cabins above the waterline

Accommodation Ladder - Portable external stairway on side of ship for shore and tender access.

Aft - Near, toward or in the rear of the ship (stern)

Air-Sea - When air transportation is part of your cruise package.

ASTA - American Society of Travel Agents.

Barter - Trading travel services for advertising. Travel service is then resold by advertising company at discounted rate.

Beam - the breadth of the ship at its widest point.

Bearing - The ships compass direction.

Berth - Dock or pier

Berth - Bed or beds in passengers cabin.

Bilge - Lowest spaces of ships innerstructure.

Bow - Front or forward portion of ship.

Bridge - Navigational & command control center of ship.

Bulkhead - Upright partition (wall) dividing the ship into cabins or compartments.

CLIA - Cruise Line International Association - Trade organization of cruise lines and travel agents.

Coaming - Raised partition at base of doorways to keep water from entering.

Colors - National Flag or ensign flown from mast or sternpost.

Companionway - Interior stairway.

Course - Direction in which ship is headed.

Debark - Getting off the ship.

Disembark - Getting off the ship.

Draft - Measurement in feet from waterline to lowest point of ships keel.

Fantail - Rear or aft overhang of ship.

Fathom - measurement of distance equal to 6 feet.

Fender - A cushion between side of ship and dock.

Forward - Toward the bow of the ship.

Free Port - A port free of customs duty and most customs regulations.

Galley - Ships kitchen

Gangway - Passageway/portable stairs by which passengers embark and disembark.

Group Rates - Usually 10-15% lower than rates listed in brochure.

Head - Toilet facilities

Inside Cabin - Cabin does not have portholes.

Knot - 1 nautical mile per hour (6080.2 ft.) as compared to land mile 5,280 ft.

Latitude - Angular distance measured in degrees north or south of the equator. One degree = approx. 60 nautical miles.

League - A measure of distance approximatly 3.45 nautical miles.

Leeward - Side of the ship/island that is protected from the wind.

Longitude - Angular distance measured in degrees east or west of the prime meridian of Greenwich, England. One degree of longitude will vary from 60 nauticl miles wide at the equator to zero at the north & south poles.

Manifest - A list or invoice of passengers, crew & cargo.

Muster - To asseble passengers/crew.

NACOA - National Association of Cruise Only Agents - Organization of travel agents who only sell cruises.

Off Season - The slow periods of the year for cruise lines.

On Season - The busy times of year for cruises. Same as Peak Season.

Outside Cabin - Cabin with porthole.

Pier Head Jump - Getting aboard a ship at the last minute before the ship sails.

Port - The left side of the ship as you look forward towards the bow.

Port Tax - Tax levied on each passenger by port authorities.

Repositioning Cruise - When a ship moves to a new cruise area for a new season.

Registry - The country in which the ship is registered.

Roll - the sway of the ship from side to side which may occur when the ship is underway.

Run of Ship - You pay a low fare and the cruise line assigns your cabin at their discretion.

SeaSavers - Discount program - You must book your cabin within 30 days of the sailing date.

Script - A piece of paper which takes the place of money in bartered trade agreements.

SeaSavers - Reduced fare program for people who book their cruise within 30 days of sailing date.

Single Occupancy -1 person in a cabin. You usually have to pay extra for single occupancy.

Stabilizers - wing like devices that swing out from the sides of the ship to produce a stable ride.

Stand By - A name list of passengers trying to get on a sold out cruise. Or passengers hoping to get on a cruise at a reduced rate (American Hawaii Standby Program).

Starboard - The right side of the ship as you look forward towards the bow.

Stem - The extreme bow of the ship.

Stern - The rear of the ship.

Stowaway - An illegal passenger.

Tender - Small vessel used to transport passengers to and from shore when ship is at anchor.

Transderm V - a band-aid patch placed behind the ear to prevent motion discomfort.

Wake - The agitated water left by the passing of a ship.

Windward - Facing into the wind.

INDEX

About the Author

A retired merchant seaman, Capt. Bill Miller has owned a cruise travel agency for several years. Capt. Miller is a longtime member of Cruise Lines International Association and the Pacific Asian Travel Agents Association.

Capt. Miller's extensive insiders knowledge of the billion dollar cruise industry makes him uniquely qualified to share cruise discount secrets.

Capt. Miller lives in St.Petersburg, Florida with his wife Susan, daughter Amy and three labrador retrievers.

THANK YOU

Dear Cruisers,

You are the true experts.

You are the pioneers who try out new cruise itineraries and new ships and new discount programs. You become the experts with the "Insiders Knowledge".

Have you got a great way to save money on cruises that you would like to share? Write to me and share your Insider Secrets! My address is P.O. Box 41005, St.Petersburg, Fl. 33743.

I will be including new information that you discover in the next edition of Insiders Guide To Cruise Discounts.

Until then,

BON VOYAGE

Capt. Bill Miller

....

"INSIDERS GUIDE TO CRUISE DISCOUNTS" is the perfect gift for your friends. Send them a copy, they will thank you for it!

Additional copies are available for $9.95 plus $2.00 for shipping and handling. To order, send your check or money order for a total of $11.95 to:

Ticket To Adventure, Inc
P.O. Box 41005
St.Petersburg, Fl. 33743

NOTES

NOTES

NOTES

NOTES